THE
ARCHITECTURAL
TREASURES
OF
EARLY AMERICA
SERIES

HISTORICAL INTRODUCTION

In 1914 the White Pine Bureau, the public relations arm of the producers of architectural grades of white pine, began publishing a remarkable series of sixteen-page booklets under the general title, *The White Pine Series of Architectural Monographs.* The organizations that sponsored the program were the Northern Pine Manufacturers' Association of Minnesota, Wisconsin, and Michigan, and the White Pine Manufacturers of Idaho. Individual lumber companies, in turn, made up the memberships of those organizations, and their dues financed the bureau's activities. The publishing venture was separated, therefore, by two giant steps from the individual financial interests of its sources of capital, a situation that contributed greatly to the editorial integrity of the publishing project.

Furthermore, none of the persons involved with any of the sponsoring companies or associations seem to have had serious editorial influence on the project. An editor was appointed, one Russell F. Whitehead, a practicing architect and former editor of the *Architectural Record* and *The Brickbuilder.* As we have worked with the monographs published under Mr. Whitehead's keen direction, we have come to admire his editorial approach. He practiced what I would call "light editing" insofar as rewriting and corrections are concerned. He relied heavily upon the initial selection of author, photographer, and illustrator, and in this he excelled. His first monograph, entitled "Colonial Cottages of Massachusetts During the Latter Half of the Seventeenth Century" (descriptive if overlong) was written by Joseph Everett Chandler, who had restored both the Paul Revere House of Boston and the "House of the Seven Gables" of Salem. Julian Buckly was the distinguished architectural photographer who illustrated the first monograph and many that followed. Through the years the selection of contributors carried out the promise of the first volume as eminent architectural writers were named to do succeeding monographs, and equally talented photographers and illustrators were paired with them.

The intention of the entire project was never disguised. Indeed, the subtitle of each monograph bore these words: "A bi-monthly publication suggesting the architectural uses of white pine and its availability today as a structural wood." Lest this sound as though each author was hired to beat the drum for building everything of white pine, let me hasten to add that very little of that sales message was ever put into any of the monographs. Occasionally, as if to pay his dues, an author might make reference to the long-lasting qualities of the material for exterior use or its fine-grained beauty for interior woodwork. But since the audience of architects and builders knew those things anyway, the author and editor may easily be forgiven this slight taint of commercialism.

What forthright commercial messages there were appeared at the end of each monograph. In the first paper, for example, an essay entitled "White Pine—Its Availability—Its Cost" followed the discussion of Massachusetts cottages. Drawing attention to the use of pine in three centuries of building in America, the "commercial" went on to point out that white pine does not "shrink, creep or crawl," which I suppose effectively removes it from the category of materials that might make bumpy noises in the night, and added that it is known also for its ability to season quickly and thoroughly. Its attributes as both structural and finishing wood were roundly praised. The message was signed by the aforementioned sponsors, associates in the White Pine Bureau.

If all this sounds like an advertisement today, then let it stand as such. We are so indebted to the foresight of the White Pine Producers that to praise their products is no more than their due for having given us such superbly written materials as the monographs, as excellent in every way as their wood. Neither do Mr. Whitehead's authors "shrink, creep or crawl." They attack their subjects, as you shall see, with vitality and good spirit, paint the picture of young America through the medium of its architecture, and add historical notation where it is important to explain the development of an area's buildings and style.

In reading the text that accompanies each set of photographs, one should remember that these writings were done between 1914 and 1940. A certain style with touches of Victorian pomposity is evident in the efforts of Mr. Whitehead's writers. It lessens to be sure, as the series progresses, but it is there to some degree in all of the writings.

Since the writing and illustration were done from thirty-five to sixty-five years ago, it is to be expected that many of the buildings shown and described are no longer in existence. It is unfortunate that we cannot expect to travel to Salem or Alexandria and see every building in the monographs. To have removed from the present work the subjects that no longer exist would have been to destroy the series. We are most fortunate to have this record of early American architecture as a guide and inspiration, because so many of the buildings that make up the main volume of its content are either no longer in existence or have been modernized beyond recognition. The closer we can get to a look at the unchanged architecture of colonial and early American days, the more we can learn about its purest forms. The Pine Monographs give us the closest look we have.

Finally, in reading the text, it is well to remember that an effort has been made to edit each monograph considerably, to make it more useful to present-day readers. We have not changed meanings, at least to our knowledge. We have eliminated passages that bore little on the subject at hand and related only to topics of the day in 1914 or 1928. We have eliminated whole sections that, in our editorial judgement, do not contribute to a genuine architectural survey of the colonies and early America. And, of course, except as reproduced and commented upon above, we have eliminated the "commercials" of the Pine Producers to whose sponsorship we are so indebted for the entirety of this work.

As a concluding historical note it should be added that the monographs continued until 1925 to be produced under the sponsorship of the bureau. In that year Weyerhauser assumed the sponsorship. In place of general white-pine "commercials," each volume contained what we would now call a "house ad" for Weyerhauser, but otherwise the series continued with the same editorial purpose, integrity, and style as before.

In 1928 the monograph series seems to have broken away from sponsorship to become a kind of independent magazine, still under the editorial auspices of Mr. Whitehead. We found advertisements for companies other than Weyerhauser, although the editorial content continued to be a single architectural survey each issue, with the same dauntless and untainted integrity that was of such obvious importance to both editor and reader.

The final change took place in 1932, when the monographs became part of a monthly magazine called *Pencil Points,* published for architects and architectural draftsmen. Several times each year an issue of *Pencil Points,* until 1940, contained monographs, which improved in style and content. The measured drawings of important features and buildings became more frequent. The photography improved, and great breadth of coverage was added in terms of geographical selection.

New England was a most logical place for the monograph authors to have begun their work when one considers that the overall purpose was to promote the use of white pine. Most early buildings in New England depended upon that material both inside and out and in the years 1914—1940 an abundance of good examples were still available in that region. After sponsorship was dropped by the producers of pine, the monographs delved into the stone and brick architecture of Pennsylvania, Maryland, and other states.

We do not know whether Mr. Whitehead, his sponsors, and authors ever conceived that their efforts might be put into one set of volumes such as this one. That they did not is evidenced by some lack of subject balance—a great deal is published here on New England, not as much as we would like on Pennsylvania and the Southern states. We hope someday to rectify that with additional volumes, which, alas, will not bear the easy editorial hand of the great Mr. Whitehead, but which we hope, in a small way, will add to the completeness of the present effort.

Robert G. Miner
Editor of Publications
The Early American Society
Harrisburg, Pennsylvania

PREFACE

Not too many months ago Robert Miner, editor of *Early American Life* magazine, told me that he and his staff were going to republish the contents of the *White Pine Series of Architectural Monographs* and asked if I had ever heard of them. "My dear sir," I was quick to respond, "I have not only heard of them, but I have used them in my work and collected them over a period of years until I had them all, then reluctantly sold my collection when a move to smaller quarters forced the dispersal of accumulated treasure."

I love crawling about in the dust of secondhand bookstores. That's the kind of place where I found my first dusty copies of a few of Mr. Whitehead's monographs. I sat down and read until the proprietor politely suggested that I might be more comfortable if I bought the little green and buff volumes and removed them to the more sanitary conditions of my home. I soon resolved to try to collect all the volumes of the entire series, not more than a few thousand of which were ever printed. It was only after many years of searching that I finally completed my set. It proved to be much more than personally satisfying reading — it was of enormous help in working with period rooms in connection with my position as a museum curator.

The last monograph appeared a couple of years before the entry of the United States in World War II. Six years later, after the war created a whole new market of potential homeowners, a general abandonment of traditional American architectural design took place. The "functional modern" became revered, and good early American design ceased to be used. There was enormous demand for low-cost housing, and new materials were being developed to allow row after row of sterile "functional-simplistic" designs to come into being.

A ground swell of yearning for traditional design seems to have caused a reversal, at least in nomenclature, back to the roots of our architectural heritage. Such interesting descriptions as "tri-level colonial split ranch" began to appear in developers' ads. Features and materials were adapted willy-nilly from one area to another without cause. A new generation of architects, it seemed, had become oblivious to the integrity of the past.

At the same time, spurred no doubt by historic site development and restoration, interest in preservation and restoration began to grow. Older buildings became sought after despite years of neglect or even partial destruction. The demand continues, and of late some developers have even begun to apply correctly the beautiful principles of early American architecture in new construction. Some architects and a few builders have copies of the old *White Pine Monographs,* but they have never been available to the public. Now all can have these immensely valuable and important papers.

I am overjoyed with the new edition of this work and applaud the rearrangement of its contents for easier reference. Like Mr. Blandings I dream of a dreamhouse, and I think there are many like me who will be able to dream better dreams as well as build better houses after reading *The Architectural Treasures of Early America.*

Eric DeJonge

THE SERIES

ARCHITECTURAL TREASURES OF EARLY AMERICA

ARCHITECTURAL TREASURES OF EARLY AMERICA

EARLY HOMES
OF
MASSACHUSETTS

From material originally published as
The White Pine Series of Architectural Monographs
edited by
Russell F. Whitehead and Frank Chouteau Brown

Prepared for this series by the staff of
The Early American Society

Robert G. Miner, Editor
Anne Annibali, Design and Production
Jeff Byers, Design and Production
Nancy Dix, Editorial Assistant
Patricia Faust, Editorial Assistant
Carol Robertson, Editorial Assistant

An
Early
American
Society
Book

Published by Arno Press Inc.

Copyright © 1977 by Arno Press Inc. and The Early American Society, Inc.

Library of Congress Cataloging in Publication Data

Main entry under title:

Early homes of Massachusetts.

    (Architectural treasures of early America ; v. 1)
(An Early American Society book)
    1.   Architecture, Domestic — Massachusetts.
2.   Architecture, Colonial — Massachusetts. 3.   Architecture —
Massachusetts. I. Miner, Robert G. II. Early American
Society. III. The Monograph series, records of
early American architecture. IV. Series.
NA7235.M4E18   728.3   77-104

ISBN: 0-405-10064-7 (Arno)   ISBN: 0-517-53235-2 (Crown)
Distributed to the book trade by Crown Publishers, Inc.

CONTENTS

EARLY HOMES
OF
MASSACHUSETTS

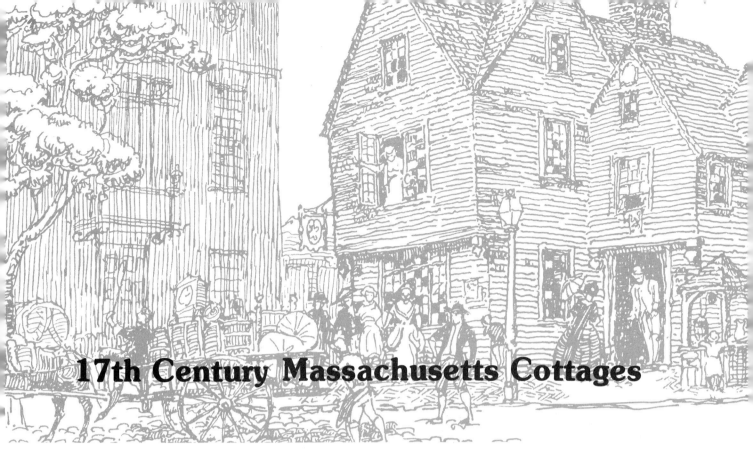

17th Century Massachusetts Cottages

Some of the early craftsmen who became our carpenter-builders in New England brought with them from the mother-country certain traditional methods of construction, and for a period followed the ways with which they were familiar. But the new country, with its rigorous climate, rapid temperature changes and frequent searching storms, as well as the completely new materials with which they were obliged to work, soon caused them to adapt their work to the new conditions, with results which were utterly distinct from any work of the mother-country.

There was not much masonry used in our early domestic architecture. The foundations were of stone, frequently laid up in clay dug from the cellars; the spaces between the timbers of the framework were filled with soft brick of home manufacture, often laid up in clay mortar; the chimneys were of stone or of brick, sometimes of the two in combination, with the hearths of the fireplaces of smooth, large stones, or of hard brick, or of large, heavy tiles brought from the mother-country.

These few portions of the house were the only ones not built of wood, for the framework, the floors and the walls alike bear testimony to the ease with which the native woods were employed to further comfort and beauty. Undoubtedly their builders gave thought to the beautiful, even in those stern days of wresting a livelihood from the new and difficult soil and the waters which isolated them from the rest of the world. Why otherwise should the summer-beams which carried the overhanging second stories have their edges chamfered, with beautiful moldings carved into the chamfer, and stopped at the ends with the familiar "lamb's-tongue" ornament? The amount of care lav-

ished on these early buildings is surprising. At the same time, had the material been oak, as it was in the English houses, it could never have been executed with the small means at the disposal of the colonists. Instead of oak the colonists used the strong, easily worked, comparatively light and entirely durable white pine, the best of the plentiful native woods. The mass of the house as well as the details was studied by their craftsmen-builders; witness the many cases where they were built with overhanging second stories on the front or sides and occasionally having the gable ends treated in a similar way. This overhang was probably reminiscent of the traditional English construction, but was unquestionably carried out because it was picturesque, and not because of its utility or ease of construction. Very frequently the overhang was embellished with brackets, drops and chamfered beams or girts, which show considerable care and a decided feeling for form in their selection.

The overhang on the front, which was a more usual position for it than on the ends of the building, generally had four carved ornamental drops depending from the four girts, two at the ends and two on the extension of the central chimney girts, when the projection of the second story was of "framed" construction and sufficient to receive them. Possibly, at times, brackets were used at either side of the front door, and certainly when gable ends projected they were frequently carried on brackets, sometimes of ornamental form, as was the case in the Capen house, in Topsfield, Massachusetts, which is in many ways one of the most interesting of the remaining examples.

The interiors likewise were not built as was most convenient, but show that care and

THE CAPEN HOUSE AT
TOPSFIELD, MASSACHUSETTS.

Built during the second half
of the 17th century;
an example of the framed overhang type.

The central bracket supporting the
gable overhang is the original;
the "drops" are restored

thought were displayed in treating the novel conditions encountered by the early builders so as to produce an interesting and often beautiful effect. For example, many of the houses had their interiors ceiled vertically with boards of random widths, inclining to be very broad, the edges matched and the juncture carrying a series of moldings which were flush with the faces of the boards. In some cases a type of decoration has been found of a curious dentil cut into these moldings, which are then run between the chimney girt and posts, on the edge of the

DETAIL OF OLD BRAY HOUSE, WEST
GLOUCESTER, MASSACHUSETTS

The corner post — "shouldered" — is roughly carved. It is a piece of ornamented construction of great interest.

18

boarding. The under flooring of the upper rooms was exposed and thereby formed a roughly paneled ceiling between the girders and joists, and this flooring was as interesting seen from above as from below, for it was made of great slabs of white pine held in place with wooden pegs. In spite of the fact that they were often two feet in width, because of the nature of the material they show little shrinkage and few cracks.

The posts, girts, summer-beams and joists were usually exposed in the interior, and were frequently of such great size that the construction might almost be called massive, although they were put together in the most characterful way, tongued and pinned and oftentimes decorated with moldings and chamfers. This construction, so direct and convincing, has a feeling quite distinct from that later work which usually comes to mind when the word "Colonial" is used, it being rather Gothic than Classic in its charm and spirit.

The inside walls were usually plastered even in the houses where the chimney end partitions were covered with wood; and as most of the early work was unpainted and left to darken with age, the flooring only being sanded or scrubbed, the combination of color was indescribably warm, rich and satisfying, and completed most satisfactorily rooms of excellent structural design. The days have happily not

DETAIL OF OLD BROWN HOUSE, HAMILTON, MASSACHUSETTS

The overhang is unusual in being a framed end showing end-girt molded and chamfered. This is a fine type of "drop" ornament depending from the posts framed into the projecting second end-girt. "The House of the Seven Gables" in Salem was found to be similar to this house.

THE FAIRBANKS HOUSE AT DEDHAM, MASS. Built in 1636
The oldest house in America (excepting possibly the shell and adobe houses of Florida and California), which is now standing, in practically its original condition. The central portion of the house is 341 years old. It was built of White Pine, left unpainted, and remains today a striking tribute to the enduring qualities of this material.

THE CORBETT HOUSE, IPSWICH, MASSACHUSETTS

(opposite page, top) Of the hewn overhang type and built during the second half of the 17th century. The gable end overhang is slight but continuous, with molded edges of framing where showing extensively. The chimney is an excellent example of the "pilastered" type belonging to this period. The fenestration is probably original as to location and size, but it is thought double-hung sash have been substituted for the single leaded sash.

THE OLD ELLERY HOUSE, GLOUCESTER, MASSACHUSETTS

(opposite page, bottom) Of the framed overhang type. Built during the second half of the 17th century. The roof has projecting gable ends with "lean-to." The chimney is larger and nearer square than is usual in this kind of house. The original "drops" from the ends of the second-story posts have been removed and small ball-shaped ornaments substituted.

THE SALTONSTALL-WHIPPLE HOUSE, IPSWICH, MASS.

Built between 1636 and 1675

Hewn end overhang type. The overhang is here entirely at the end of the house, and in both the second story and attic. The chimney is a good example of this period, with projection at back, indicating early additions to it when the "lean-to" was added. The windows have been restored according to legend with triple sash, but the panes of glass should not be divided by wood muntins, but rather with lead. The house is one of the claimants against the Fairbanks House for the distinction of being the oldest house now standing in America. It was undoubtedly, however, built at a later date.

gone by when many people consider this kind of an interior much more attractive than one in which the walls are covered with elaborate work and painted innumerable coats, rubbed down and glossed to a "piano finish." There is at least one recent instance where an owner has built his home in the form of this early period, leaving the marks of the adze and other implements on the wood, following the old methods of construction carefully, the result being a modern house thoroughly American in spirit and of old-time honesty and charm of feeling.

These houses were in many ways different from the later and better known Colonial type on the exterior as well as within ; the roofs were steeper, the houses thinner, and what little detail there was, was of forms founded on Domestic Gothic work rather than on those of the period of the Classic Revival ; the chimneys usually were long and comparatively thin, instead of massive and square as we should have expected, and were frequently embellished by projecting pilasters. An example of this sort of chimney may be seen in the Boardman House at Saugus, as well as in the Corbett House at Ipswich.

The green and white of the conventional Colonial was likewise a thing of later development, for many of the old houses have never had a coat of paint. Others were probably not

painted until many years after their construction, and the fact that so many of the older buildings have remained in good condition until this day, without any paint at all, is extraordinary testimony to the durability of the materials used in their construction.

These houses, built in the stress of strenuous early times, do not furnish us much for study or emulation in the way of detail, except that most admirable kind which was applied to the important constructional pieces of framing. These forms are so different from those we usually employ and are of such honesty and charm that they deserve to be far more extensively known than is the case at present. Therefore it seems appropriate this Series commence with the depiction of these early efforts of house-building in one of the foremost and most individual of the original States, and from which early domestic architecture gradually evolved that type which is commonly referred to to-day as the Colonial Style.

THE OLD BRAY HOUSE AT WEST GLOUCESTER, MASSACHUSETTS

An example of the hewn overhang type of construction. The large size of the cornice would suggest that a plaster cove cornice had once been used here.

THE OLD LOW HOUSE, WENHAM, MASSACHUSETTS

The original house was built in the second half of the 17th century, with framed overhang, front and side. In the 18th century the addition in front of this was added, the chimneys both being of this latter period. The house is a picturesque growth and combination of the two periods.

THE CAPEN HOUSE, TOPSFIELD, MASSACHUSETTS

An example of the framed overhang type built during the second half of the 17th century. The ''drops'' were restored after the Brown house at Hamilton, Massachusetts. The bracket in the center of the gable overhang is the original one; those at the sides of the doorway are reproduced from this, and are a sensible embellishment, but not as constructional as the girt-supported posts and the drops usual in this position. The use of ''drop'' ornaments in the gable is questionable. The fenestration has been unchanged in restoration, although leaded sash have been substituted in place of ''double-hung'' sash.

THE OLD BOARDMAN HOUSE, SAUGUS, MASSACHUSETTS

SEVENTEENTH-CENTURY HOUSE WHICH HAS NEVER BEEN PAINTED

THE JOHN WARD HOUSE
SALEM, MASSACHUSETTS.

The exact date of the unpainted White Pine siding is not known, but there are records making certain that the siding on the main portion of the house is from 150 to 200 years old, and stands now as originally built with practically no repair. Although the siding of the lean-to is of a much later date, one is unable to notice an appreciable difference between it and that put on almost two hundred years ago.

From the Mary H. Northend Collection, Salem, Mass.

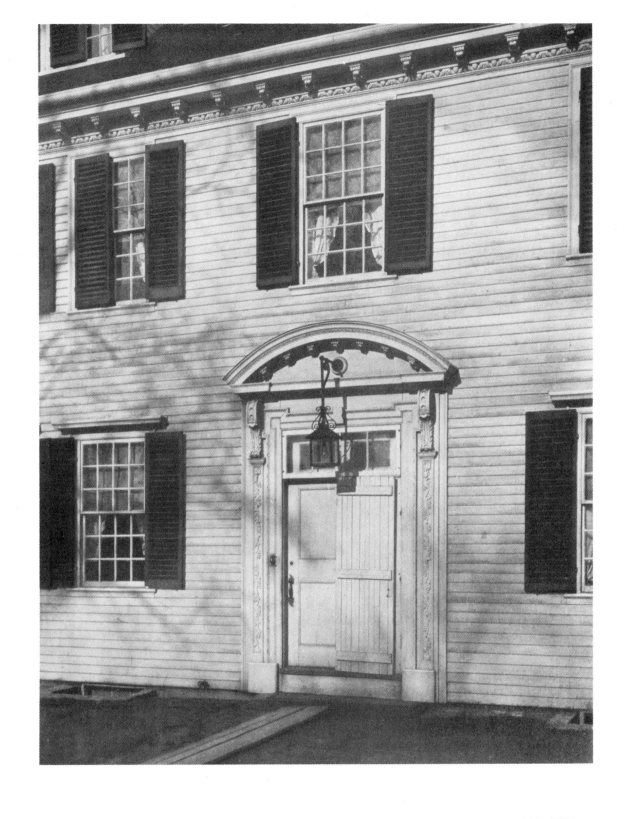

THE GOVERNOR WILLIAM DUMMER HOUSE AT BYFIELD, MASSACHUSETTS.
Detail of Entrance and Front Façade.

The doorway is almost Jacobean in character, which is a type seldom found in this vicinity.

Newburyport, Massachusetts

THE city of Newburyport lies a few miles up-stream from the mouth of the river Merrimack, which forms its harbour, and was, at one period of its early and greater days, second in importance only to Boston among New England seaports. This was in the early years of the nineteenth century, when Massachusetts ships were to be seen in most of the harbours of the world; in the year 1804 it is recorded that the duties collected in Massachusetts exceeded even those of New York. This was the time when Newburyport was at the height of its prosperity, the receipts of its Custom House ranking third among Massachusetts ports of entry, and its imports in a single month reaching the value of more than three-quarters of a million dollars. In the year 1805 its fleet numbered one hundred and seventy-three ships and other vessels of good size, exclusive of smaller craft not listed. Shipbuilding was also an important industry there, and at one period one hundred vessels were under construction at the same time. A number of frigates and sloops of war were built in its yards, and later on some of the swift clipper ships, such as the renowned "Dreadnought," that made the American merchant marine famous. One generally hears that Newburyport was founded in 1635, but, strictly speaking, that is the date of settlement of the town of Newbury, from which Newburyport was set off in the middle of the eighteenth century. The two towns still form one community in a geographical and social sense. The original settlement was not on the Merrimack, but on the shores of the Parker River, a

smaller tidal stream lying a mile or two farther toward the South. The early settlers formed a farming community, but the proximity of the Merrimack led naturally to the upbuilding of sea trade, and long before the time of the Revolution it had become a shipping centre of considerable importance. Its traffic was largely with England and the continent of Europe, while that of Salem was more with the East Indies, a difference having its origin, it is said, in the limitation set on the size of Newburyport ships by the depth of water over the bar at the harbour mouth. The East India trade demanded larger ships than Newburyport could furnish, so Salem and Portsmouth were able to develop this important trade at the expense of the town on the Merrimack.

While there are interesting buildings in all parts of the town, the chief architectural interest of Newburyport lies in its High Street, which, wide and straight, and shaded by elm trees throughout its length of three miles, is one of the most charming streets to be found anywhere in New England. It lies along "The Ridge," a gentle rise of land roughly parallel to the river, and many of the old houses on its upper side stand on terraces well above the street and have deep gardens behind them running back to pasture and farm land beyond. A most interesting view of the town may be had from the rear of some of the places on the upper side of the High Street. Many of the gardens have in them little arbours or summer houses of lattice-work, that are as old as the houses themselves. Several of the more important gardens, especially those that are terraced, are of considerable interest and charm. One passing through the town is impressed by the large number of great, square three-storied houses whose dignified aspect testifies to the prosperity and good taste of their builders of a hundred years ago and more. The houses of this type were built, for the most part, between the Revolution and the War of 1812, few of them antedating the Declaration of Independence. Among the earliest and finest of the houses of this type are the Lowell-Johnson house and the Jackson-Dexter house, both in the High Street. The latter house was the residence of that eccentric merchant who called himself "Lord" Timothy Dexter, around whose name various legends have accumulated, among them the story of a shipload of warming-pans sent to the West Indies, where they were sold at great profit as ladles for use in sugar refineries. An old print shows how this house looked in Timothy Dexter's time, when it had a sort of forecourt between it and the street, around which were ranged on high pedestals a number of wooden statues representing George Washington, Benjamin Franklin, John Hancock and other historical worthies, together with several mythological characters and a number of animals.

While houses of the square, three-storied type are undoubtedly what give its predominant character to the town, there are notable examples of the two-storied gambrel-roof type as well, of which the Bradbury-Spalding house in Green Street, built about 1790, is one of the best. Much older is the house in State Street now occupied by the Dalton Club. It is not known just when this was built, but its builder, Michael Dalton, bought the land in 1746, which would place the date of its erection later, at all events, than that. The boarding of the front is coursed in imitation of stone. The interior finish is very good and there is a particularly fine staircase with twisted newels and balusters. It was in this house that George Washington stayed when on his journey through the New England States. An unusual feature of this house is the great breadth of its façade, which made it possible to have five dormers in the roof without any sense of crowding.

THE JAMES NOYES HOUSE, NEWBURY, MASSACHUSETTS.
Built in 1646. The doorways are additions made about 1830.

THE JONATHAN PLUMMER HOUSE, NEWBURY OLDTOWN, MASSACHUSETTS.　Built in 1760.

THE NELSON-WHEELWRIGHT HOUSE, NEWBURYPORT, MASSACHUSETTS.
An example of the smaller three-story house.　The porch is obviously modern.

THE THOMAS HALE HOUSE, 348 HIGH STREET, NEWBURYPORT, MASSACHUSETTS.

A very dignified three-story house.   Both the porch and the fence are original.

THE KNAPP-PERRY HOUSE, 47 HIGH STREET, NEWBURYPORT, MASSACHUSETTS.

Built in 1809. The wooden fence corresponds in design with railing around the deck of the house.

Entrance Detail.
HOUSE AT 27 HIGH ST., NEWBURYPORT, MASSACHUSETTS.

The type of doorway originally on the gambrel-roofed house,
now largely replaced by doorways of the Neo-Grec period.

Entrance Detail.
THE EMERY HOUSE, 252 HIGH ST.,
NEWBURYPORT, MASSACHUSETTS.

Built in 1796 by Thomas Coker.   The transom is
brought forward and painted like the woodwork.

THE MOULTON HOUSE, NEWBURYPORT, MASSACHUSETTS.   Built *circa* 1810.

A stately example of the three-story Newburyport house.
The houses along the Ridge are of similar type.

Porch, No. 68 High Street, Newburyport, Massachusetts
THE STOREY-WALTERS HOUSE.   1801.
Built by Samuel Sweet.

THE SAWYER-HALE HOUSE, NEWBURYPORT, MASSACHUSETTS
Built during the latter part of the 18th century. Particularly
good cornice, dormer spacing, and broken scroll pediment.

Porch, No. 348 High Street, Newburyport, Massachusetts.
THE THOMAS HALE HOUSE. 1800.
The columns rest on round reeded pedestals.

THE SHORT HOUSE, NEWBURY, MASSACHUSETTS.   Built in 1717.
Detail of Doorway.

These are among the oldest panelled doors in New England.

THE SHORT HOUSE, NEWBURY, MASSACHUSETTS. Built in 1717.

A two-storied house of the older type with plain pitched roof and large square chimney in each gable end.

A still older type of two-storied house having a plain pitched roof is the Short house, No. 6 High Street, Newbury, which was built soon after 1717, when the land was acquired by Nathaniel Knight, and is given an unusual character by the large square chimney in each gable, the gable ends of the house being of brick. The front door of this house is of a kind unusual in that part of the country, with its pair of doors and the narrow light over them. These doors are undoubtedly the original ones and are of interest on that account, as few existing outside doors in old houses are of the period of the house itself. In many cases, not only the doors, but their architectural framework as well, have been replaced by later ones much inferior in design and detail to the rest of the building, so that one often sees on houses that obviously date from the eighteenth century, doorways of the pseudo-Greek type of 1830.

In the neighbouring town of Byfield, which was formerly Byfield parish of the town of Newbury, is the very interesting old house which is now the residence of the head-master of Dummer Academy. Its main entrance is unlike any other in the neighbourhood, its pilasters being ornamented with grape-vines carved in quite high relief, and carrying carved brackets which support the pediment.

THE BRADBURY-SPALDING HOUSE, NEWBURYPORT, MASSACHUSETTS.

Built, *circa* 1790, by Theophilus Bradbury An especially good example of the gambrel roof, three-dormer type. The doorway has splayed jambs, a characteristic feature of Newburyport houses.

In Newbury and Oldtown and the outlying portions of Newburyport are numerous farmhouses of the simple and dignified type found almost everywhere in New England, but the individual character of Newburyport is chiefly given by the square three-storied "Mansion Houses," of which so many are found in the High Street.

Newburyport, although to-day manufacturing has taken the place of sea-borne commerce as its chief industry, is less changed than most other old towns of its importance, and one can easily form a good idea of how it must have looked in the year 1800 when Timothy Dwight, President of Yale College, visited it while on a tour through the New England States, after which visit he wrote:

"The houses, taken collectively, make a better appearance than those of any other town in New England. Many of them are particularly handsome. Their appendages, also, are unusually neat. Indeed, an air of wealth, taste and elegance is spread over this beautiful spot with a cheerfulness and brilliancy to which I know no rival. . . . Upon the whole, few places probably in the world furnish more means of a delightful residence than Newburyport."

"LORD" TIMOTHY DEXTER HOUSE, NEWBURYPORT, MASSACHUSETTS. Built about 1772.
Showing the house as it at present stands in the High Street after the removal of the forecourt and statues.

THE FOSTER HOUSE, NEWBURYPORT, MASSACHUSETTS.
Built about 1808. Note the wide corner-boards, the interesting treatment of the deck and detail of the dormers

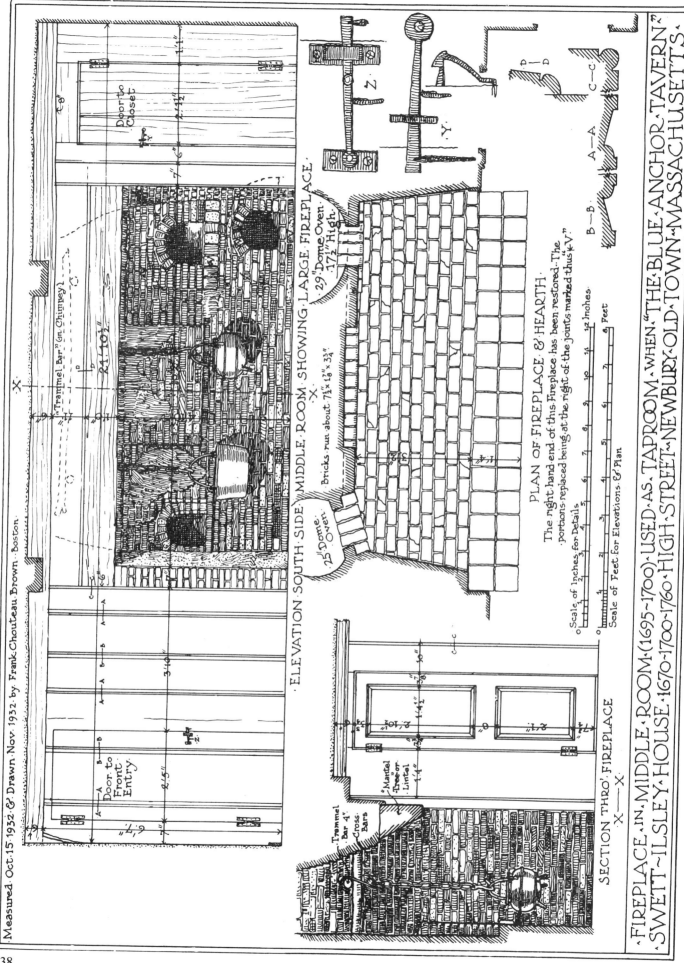

Measured. Oct. 15. 1932. & Drawn. Nov. 1932. by. Frank. Chouteau. Brown. Boston.

Door to Closet

Door to Front Entry.

"Trammel Bar" (in Chimney)

29" Dome Oven 17½" High.

25" Dome Oven

Bricks run about 7¼" × 18" × 3¾"

· ELEVATION · SOUTH · SIDE · MIDDLE · ROOM · SHOWING · LARGE · FIREPLACE ·
· X ·

PLAN · OF · FIREPLACE · & · HEARTH.

The right hand end of this Fireplace has been restored. The portions replaced being at the right of the joints marked thus "V."

Scale of Inches for Details

Scale of Feet for Elevations & Plan

"Mantel Tree" or Lintel

Trammel Bar 4' Cross Bars

· SECTION · THRO' · FIREPLACE ·
· X · X ·

A—A

B—B

C—C

· FIREPLACE · IN · MIDDLE · ROOM · (1695~1700) · USED · AS · TAPROOM · WHEN · "THE · BLUE · ANCHOR · TAVERN"?
· SWETT ~ ILSLEY · HOUSE · 1670~1700~1760 · HIGH · STREET ~ NEWBURY · OLD · TOWN · MASSACHUSETTS ·

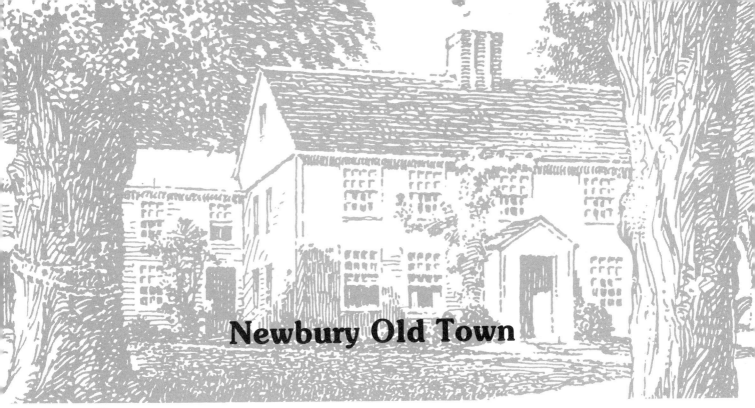

Newbury Old Town

Continuing further to trace the gradual development of our early domestic architecture in the Eastern settlements during the Seventeenth Century, we may turn to the older section of Newbury, Massachusetts, to provide some pertinent and definite illustrations. The early small two-room story-and-a-half cottage, with chimney at one end, was soon supplanted by the full two-story house with end chimney —as in the original portions of the Coffin and Swett dwellings at "Ould Newbury," dating from about 1653 and 1670, respectively.

Both types were soon enlarged, by adding other rooms beyond the chimneys; or in some of the ways particularly described herewith—or they were supplanted by the larger plan, with central chimney and staircase against its southern face, with living "Hall" at one side, and the principal family sleeping chamber at the other. This obvious and simple arrangement was soon supplemented by the separate kitchen at the back of the chimney—usually in a leanto at the rear.

Next, one or both of the end spaces might be divided into two rooms—the rear ones upon the second floor being reached by another stairway in the "leanto"; and then the plans' final amplification might be made by substituting end chimneys for the large central one, thus allowing the central hallway to extend through the house to reach the rear as well as the front rooms, upon both upper and lower floors.

Among these Newbury Old Town dwellings, the Jackman-Willett house itself illustrates the next step beyond the original Riggs house at Riverdale, in the story-and-a-half cottage—now with three rooms upon the ground floor; while the Tristram Coffin house shows—although with a difference, itself almost unique!—the favorite method of adding a new and fully developed plan upon one end of the earlier southern-fronted cottage, leaving it to func-

tion as a kitchen ell, and establishing a new frontage to either east or west, toward a main highway. And, finally, the Swett-Ilsley grouping shows a more extensive arrangement of an early house extension, as in the Riggs dwelling, but here that process has been extended over a period of fully a hundred and fifty years, while at the same time changing the direction of growth.

It was in 1634 that the Rev. Thomas Parker, of Newbury in Old England, arrived in New England with Nicholas Noyes, John Spencer and nearly an hundred other followers, on the "Mary and John." They made their "landing" on the shores of the Quascacunquen, now the Parker, River; very near where the "Old Bay Road" from Ipswich to Newburyport now crosses that stream—and the earliest settlement was upon the northern bank, although in 1642 most of the settlers removed to more fertile land a few miles further northward, where each freeholder was given a "house lot of 4 akers," in the area still known as "Newbury Old Town." And here the original Noyes home still stands, near the "Lower Green," although it has been so added to and changed —both within and without—that little remains to substantiate its early date (of about 1645 or '46) except its huge timbers and summers, themselves largely out of sight above the lowered plaster ceilings added in later years.

Along with the Spencer-Pierce house, now usually known as the Little House, nearby—but of an ancient character still apparent despite the changes and additions that were made some hundred or more years ago—it is probably the most ancient among the early dwellings of this old part of Newbury. But the latter's cross-shaped plan; its thick stone walls, and old kitchen chimney (at the end of what is the northern arm of the cross—the southern portion being the

39

THE RICHARD DOLE-LITTLE HOUSE—1670—NEWBURY OLD TOWN, MASSACHUSETTS

unusual brick gable or "Porch") make it unique among Massachusetts early house architecture—its nearest counterpart being probably the "Old Stone House" (1640) at Guilford, Conn. It, too, was probably built very near 1645 by either the original holder, John Spencer—or it may have been a few years later, by one Daniel Pierce, who bought the land of John Spencer's son in 1651.

Not only was the Coffin family prolific in the number of its human descendants, but also in its architectural products, as well. Tristram, the first of that name in the new world, was an old Royalist, who arrived in Haverhill, Massachusetts, from Brixton, Devonshire, in 1642, and first settled at Salisbury, near the mouth of the Merrimac. In December, 1647, he was granted the ferry privilege at "Newbury side," as well as keeping an "Ordinary," or Inn. But by 1653 the original part of the present Tristram Coffin structure, a two-story building with one room on the first floor and two on the second, with a chimney at its eastern end—now a part of the rearmost section of the house—was certainly in existence; as on March 2 of that year his son, Tristram, Jr., married Mrs. Somersby (née Judith Greenleaf) a widow, and was living there. It is even possible that this may have been a still earlier structure—belonging to the widow herself!

Meanwhile, his father, Tristram Coffin, Sr., removed to Nantucket in 1659 or 60; and there the name of the family has been perpetuated on what is now the oldest house on the Island, the Jethro Coffin house, built about 1686.

The original house had faced south, as was usual, with its doorway in front of the chimney near its eastern corner. Tristram, Jr., died Feb. 4, 1704, aged 72 years, and in his will left his "dwelling hous" to his son Nathaniel. About 1693 the frame of another building was moved up to within 13 or 14 feet of the easterly end of the older house, and what is the southeastern portion of the new front part of the dwelling was finished off, the old chimney rebuilt —or torn down and built anew—along with the intermediate portion necessary to connect the two sections. It is the fireplace in this chimney, and this room, that is shown in the measured drawing and accompanying photographs, though some of the finish may be of a still later date.

There seems to be some doubt whether the entire eastern front plan, as it appears now, was built at this time; or whether the central hallway and door in the middle of the street front, along with the rooms at the right or northern end of this new frontage were added at the time of the marriage of Nathaniel's son, Joseph, on July 15, 1725. In that event, the finish of the

40

room shown here might have been renewed either then, or possibly shortly after Nathaniel's death, when 80 years old, on February 20, 1749.

Finally, either in 1725—or at some subsequent period before 1785—there was added a room at the back or northerly side of the original house to make a kitchen for the new front northerly portion; just as the rooms at the east and west of the oldest chimney were also in use as kitchens to serve the—at least!—three Coffin families that were simultaneously living in the old homestead!

The girt, in front of the fireplace, is paralleled by another exposed a few feet beyond the western side of the same chimney, showing the portions that were added to these two rooms when the chimney was rebuilt and the two sections connected; while a slight bend in the southern length of the present building suggests to the careful observer that something a little out of the usual had probably here taken place. It is this intermediate section that is unusual—almost unique—in the records of enlarging early Colonial dwellings! While another unique feature is to be found in the old "Buttery" contained within the front portion of the dwelling, which has remained undisturbed from its original upfitting for almost two hundred years.

The other most interesting local dwelling is the Swett-Ilsley House—now again a hostelry!—which represents the changing backgrounds of over a hundred and fifty years in its various additions, without—as it fortunately happens—any of the later additions much obscuring or changing the work that had gone before. Along with the Tristram Coffin House, it is now owned by the "Society for the Preservation of New England Antiquities," and therefore its preservation is assured—barring only the unfortunate accident of fire—for many years yet to come.

The building now faces east, fronting closely on the "Old Bay Road," or High Street, only a few hundred feet beyond the more retired Coffin homestead. It has two front doorways, the one to the left admitting to the older portion. The two rooms on the first and second floors—at the left of and beyond this doorway—were the original house, then fronting south, with chimney at the west end and doorway and stairs to the south of it, in the southwest corner, with a slight front second-story overhang.

The ridgepole then ran from east to west; and this portion was built by Stephen Swett, at least as early as 1670. It may even have been several years older than that, as the chamfers on the timbers are very like those in the oldest part of the Coffin house. The frame shows where two and three mullion casement windows were set, one of these being about where the fireplace and chimney are now on the north side of the old "Hall."

The next and most important change was made previous to 1700, probably between 1690 and 1695, when what is now the middle room was built at the north of the older house, with a chimney between the old part and the addition. A new stairway was built against the eastern face of this chimney. The old west chimney was torn down; and a small corner fireplace built against the west side of the new chimney to heat the small room that occupied the space previously taken by chimney and staircase; and the ridgepole was changed to run from north to south instead of from east to west, as it had originally. The rear (west) "leanto" was built on, probably between 1756 and 1760, to provide a new kitchen back of the large "Hall," with its enormous fireplace, one of the largest of the period now known in Massachusetts. And it is this room, or rather its south side with its unusual large fireplace, that is shown in detail in the measured drawing.

This middle room with its enormous fireplace has in its rear or western end a door and sashed opening that formerly connected with the serving "bar," during that portion of the structure's existence when it was in use as the Blue Anchor Tavern; this room then being the Tap Room, and the room in the leanto behind being the Kitchen—in substantiation of which arrangement there still exists built into the front angle of this space, the remains of the old wall cupboard, of which the intermediate Kitchen of the Coffin House still shows so good an example, the invariable adjunct of the Seventeenth Century Kitchen!

The house did not come into the possession of the Ilsley family until 1797. Meanwhile, during, and for a while previous to, the Revolution, it had served as an Inn; seen the training of local companies of militia; watched the progress of the French and Indian wars (the Merrimac River being really the northern frontier of the New England settlements at that time) and

THE NOYES HOUSE—ABOUT 1645— NEWBURY OLD TOWN, MASSACHUSETTS

had at least one owner, John March, who was a captain in the attack on Canada in 1700, and later helped defend the Casco Bay fort against the French.

Still further to the north, the door, hallway, and room at its right, is the last addition that was made to the old dwelling—probably shortly after 1800. Fortunately this was accomplished without any more disturbance than the closing of a few windows and the opening of a doorway into what then became the middle room, on both lower and upper floors.

While to the more curious, there is always in reserve the attic; that space that—in New England—has so often been kept inviolate, sacred to the housewives' desire for "order," to which proscribed precincts anything outmoded or otherwise cluttering up the daily wheels of progress may always be exiled. There, amid dust and these ancient family treasures, the timber framing and changes in the house's history usually lie plainly outspread before any interested or trained observer.

Down nearer the original "landing," on the Parker River, are two old structures also worthy attention. One, the Richard Dole-Little House, is the simple long leanto dwelling, that still looks down toward the banks of the Parker River. Inside it has been much changed about to keep up with the progress and needs of its various families of occupants, but outside it certainly continues to look its years, from 1670,

the date of its beginnings.

A little further north, at a sharp turn in the road, is the Samuel Seddon house; once another "Ordinary" on the highroad out of Boston. Built in 1728, its windows are now shuttered; its old central chimney has been taken out and replaced by two smaller ones, in order to gain the room for a central hallway upon the second floor; and its floors are gradually settling and sagging out of true. But, inside, it is still possible to trace the location of the "bar," opening into the Taproom at the left, from near the rear line of the house, though if even this record is to be much longer preserved, steps must soon be taken to maintain the old frame and make the roof tight.

About midway from this old Tavern to the center of Old Newbury, at the left side of the Old Post Road, is the location of the original Burying Ground, and beside it now is the Jackman-Willett house.

Richard Jackman was the youngest son of James Jackman, the immigrant, who died in 1694, when Richard had been married thirteen years. When his father's estate was settled the following year, he built his new house, which was finished in 1696. He had married Elizabeth Plummer, and when her father—who had the ferry at the Parker River—died in 1702, Corporal Richard Jackman was appointed, on September 16, 1702, to "keep the ferry over Oldtown river, alias ye River Parker." At that time he was living in

THE DR. PETER TOPPAN HOUSE—1697—NEWBURY OLD TOWN, MASSACHUSETTS

THE SPENCER-PIERCE-LITTLE HOUSE—1650—
NEWBURY, MASSACHUSETTS *Entrance Detail*

THE JACKMAN-WILLETT HOUSE—1696—
NEWBURY OLD TOWN, MASSACHUSETTS

his new house, on a lot on the "Ferry Road," across the street from the Seddon place.

By the summer of 1930 the little house had become so dilapidated that, when the "Sons and Daughters of the First Settlers of Newbury" undertook to put it into repair, as the oldest surviving primitive cottage then available, it was decided to move it a mile or so up the Post road to a position beside the original Burying Ground, about midway between the "Landing" and the "Lower Green." The cottage probably still shows its original outlines, though the work on the interior had not been completed at the time these pictures were taken. The old chimney had not then been rebuilt, but the quaint window trim and heads, the clapboarding and "jet" finish had been carried out along the old lines, so that a very good idea of the appearance of one of the simpler types of early cottage-houses of this locality is there to be obtained.

Again continuing north toward the "Lower Green" and "the Port," the Dr. Peter Toppan house, of 1697, may be seen almost directly across the Highway from the Swett-Ilsley place. It displays one of the most imposing "gambrels" of the locality, although the walls have been covered with new shingles, and the dwelling —for some time housing two families—has but recently been brought back to its single family appearance. Probably it could assume a well deserved place in a sequential record illustrating the development of the New England gambrel roof; but, located so closely adjacent to the Swett-Ilsley and Tristram Coffin houses, it cannot but be preferably grouped with them; leaving only the better known and distinctively different architecture of the Short House waiting for some later—and fuller—presentation; which, perhaps along with the Spencer-Pierce-Little house, its beauty and individuality entitle it to receive.

Stairway

THE SWETT-ILSLEY HOUSE—1670-1700-1760—HIGH STREET, NEWBURY OLD TOWN, MASSACHUSETTS

Fireplace in Middle Room (1695-1700)

Fireplace

45

THE TRISTRAM COFFIN HOUSE—1651-1693-1725—NEWBURY OLD TOWN, MASSACHUSETTS

BUTTERY   BEDROOM

Fireplace Side of "Hall" or Kitchen (Added About 1693)

Dresser Side of "Hall" or Kitchen (Added About 1693)

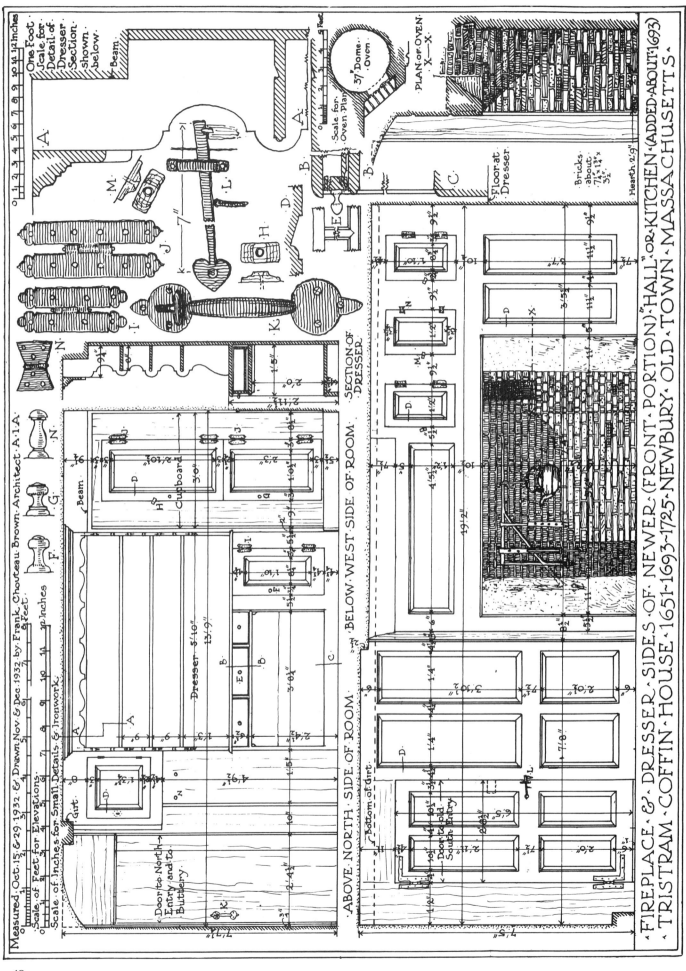

FIREPLACE & DRESSER · SIDES · OF · NEWER · (FRONT · PORTION) "HALL" · OR · KITCHEN · (ADDED · ABOUT 1693)
TRISTRAM · COFFIN · HOUSE · 1651~1693~1725 · NEWBURY · OLD · TOWN · MASSACHUSETTS ·

SOUTH ELEVATION—OLDER REAR PORTION
THE "KING" HOOPER MANSION, MARBLEHEAD, MASSACHUSETTS

FRANKLIN STREET, MARBLEHEAD, MASSACHUSETTS.
Showing the way in which the houses are generally built on the street line.

A HOUSE ON STATE STREET, MARBLEHEAD, MASSACHUSETTS.

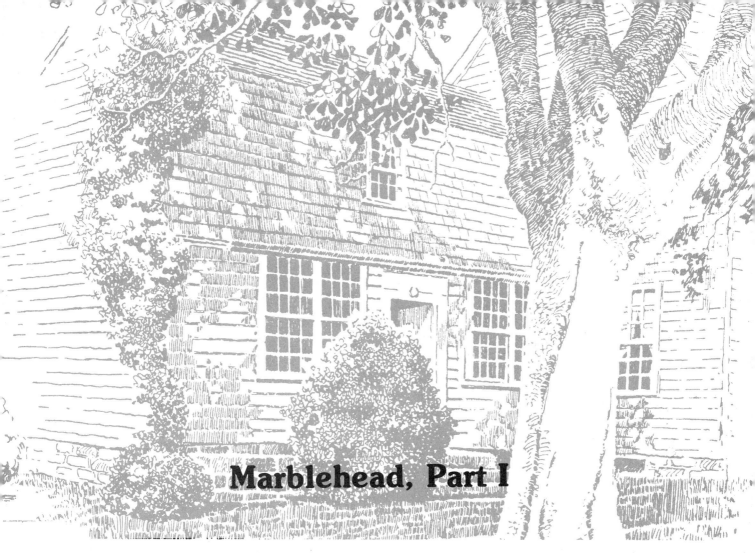

Marblehead, Part I

FROM the time of the earliest settlement in
1629 the townsmen of Marblehead, Massachusetts, have shown qualities, in times
of hardship and stress, of a very high order.
Wars, sickness, fires and storms have all at various times sorely tried this little community and
have developed a people justly distinguished for
their fortitude and courage. The daily familiar-
ity with danger and suffering of the men in the
fishing fleet made a splendid training for the
part they were to play in the wars of the Revolution and of 1812, and the pride in this tradition of service was nobly sustained by the later
generations in the time of the Civil War. Nor
are the men of to-day one bit less patriotic and
willing to do their share. Out of all proportion
to its size and wealth has been Marblehead's
contribution to the store of early American history and legend, and the names of many of its
men and women are part of the country's best
heritage.

Salem is but four miles away and of course
has somewhat eclipsed in popular interest its
smaller neighbor, and the splendor of its Colonial architecture of the early nineteenth century
has appealed to the imagination of architects
and laymen more strongly than the humbler
dwellings of the near-by town. But there is a
tremendous amount of material to be found on
the hilly, rocky peninsula of Marblehead, not
only to satisfy the seeker for picturesqueness and

literary associations, but also for the study of
early American architecture. While the peninsula which is called Marblehead is about four
miles long and from two miles to a mile and a
half wide, the town itself, where almost all the
old buildings are to be found, is perhaps two
miles long by half a mile wide and extends along
the harbor side. The site is very hilly and
irregular and the coast-line very rocky. So the
streets must needs wander about in a most delightfully casual way, and the houses must face
every which way and the yards both back and
front are necessarily restricted and form most
charming terraces and gardens. The same characteristic steep streets descending to the water
and tiers of houses rising above one another that
have given Genoa and Naples and Quebec so
much of their charm are here repeated on a
smaller scale. The houses, while they are all
free-standing, as befits this sturdy and independent people, are nevertheless built closely to
gether for their mutual comfort and neighborli-
ness. The irregularities of site have resulted in
a greater variety of plan in many of the houses
than can be met with in most of our New England communities, where the town sites are almost uniformly flat.

As seen from the harbor or from the causeway
that connects Marblehead Neck with the mainland, the silhouette of the town presents a picture
unrivalled in this country for beauty of sky-line.

THE LEE MANSION, MARBLEHEAD, MASSACHUSETTS. Entrance Porch Detail.

Formerly the home of Col. Jeremiah Lee. This house is now in the possession of the Marblehead Historical Society, and is filled with mementos of historical value.

There is no New England town which shows so many old houses in a single *coup d'oeil*.

The most prevalent type of house is the wooden clapboard one with gable or gambrel roof and generous brick chimneys. Even the more pretentious houses on Washington Street are of wood; in fact, there are only five or six old houses to be found that are built of brick. While there are several houses dating from before 1700, there is not one whose exterior aspect remains in a form typical of the seventeenth century, and not one like the House of Seven Gables in Salem, or the Cooper-Austin house in Cambridge, which immediately attracts the visitor's attention as an example of the earliest period of Colonial. By far the greatest number of dwellings date from the period of Marblehead's greatest prosperity, the middle of the eighteenth century.

Although the houses near Abbot Hall and on Washington Street are large and in a sense pretentious, and the Lee Mansion is one of the finest mansions in New England of its period, in general it is the homes of people of modest and humble circumstances that leave the most permanent impress on the memory of the observer. Even the richer houses are almost entirely devoid of carved ornaments and any elaboration of detail. In a word, austerity is the distinguishing characteristic of building in Marblehead.

But it must not be thought that bareness and monotony are the necessary accompaniments of this very democratic simplicity so expressive of what we like to think is or was the best side of American character. I believe nowhere will there be found more varieties of gables, cornices and doorways, or better examples of interior finish and panelling.

The gambrel roofs vary in angles from very steep and narrow to certain examples of low, wide gambrels, where one wonders how the flatter pitches can be kept from leaking. In the same way a designer may find precedent for gable roofs from twenty degrees all the way up to sixty degrees inclination. There are very

few hipped roofs. The two Lee houses both boast of exceedingly effective cupolas and the Col. Jeremiah Lee Mansion is embellished with a pediment on its main façade. Otherwise the roofs of Marblehead are of a soul-satisfying simplicity; even dormers are a great rarity, the few there are being later additions, with the exception of the house on Mechanic Street. The heavily moulded dormers in the gambrel roof are probably of the same date as the house. There are, on the most interesting old Governor Bradford house in Bristol, Rhode Island, three dormers in a gambrel roof that are almost identical in size and detail with the Marblehead examples, and both houses are of about the same date.

A HOUSE ON THE SEA FRONT, MARBLEHEAD, MASSACHUSETTS.
Back of this austere old house appears a bit of Marblehead's harbor, which is one of the finest along the New England shore.

THE LEE MANSION, MARBLEHEAD, MASSACHUSETTS.

Built in 1768 by Col. Jeremiah Lee. Its original cost is said to have been ten thousand pounds. It is still noted for its excellent hall and stairway.

HOUSE ON WASHINGTON STREET, MARBLEHEAD, MASSACHUSETTS.

THE BOWEN HOUSE, MARBLEHEAD, MASSACHUSETTS.
One of the oldest houses in the town. It is situated on the corner of Mugford
Street near the Town House. A glimpse is afforded of the irregularity of the land.

Detail of Entrance Porch.
HOUSE ON WASHINGTON ST., MARBLEHEAD, MASSACHUSETTS.

Doorway
HOUSE ON FRANKLIN STREET, MARBLEHEAD,
MASSACHUSETTS.
It appears that the hall wainscoting cap has been repeated on
the pilasters on the outside of the main entrance.

Detail of Entrance Vestibule.
HOUSE ON WASHINGTON ST., MARBLEHEAD, MASSACHUSETTS.

HOUSE ON TUCKER STREET, MARBLEHEAD, MASSACHUSETTS.

The older cornices are simple as can be, and are without any decorative feature; but later there is a fascinating variety of moulded cornices with dentils and modillions all worthy of careful study. What a lesson this town teaches in the value of cornices of small projection and few members.

Clapboards cover the walls of almost every building, but we find several instances of wood boarding cut to imitate stone in a simple rusticated pattern, on all sides as on the Lee mansion, and only on the front as on the King Hooper house. Corner boards are the rule, varying from four to eight inches in width.

The exterior window trims vary greatly and are of great interest. In many cases the second-story trims are charmingly composed with the bed mouldings of the cornice. Often the first-story windows have little cornices of their own. The very satisfying quality of the window sashes and blinds is due to careful thought by some one in years gone by, and they can be most profitably studied by modern designers.

The Doric order was evidently invented for Marblehead, as all but two or three of the front entrances are adorned with it in the form of column or pilaster. The two Lee houses flaunt the gay Ionic, and on Franklin Street there are two extraordinary doorways of the early nineteenth century flanked by delightfully quaint pilasters of a curious composite type, tapering downward to their plinths. Especially interesting, too, is the enclosed entrance porch on a house in Lookout Court, with its elliptical fanlight, reeded pilasters and grooved ornaments. So many of the houses are built on the sidewalk line that there are many interesting examples of recessed doorways with the steps in the recess. The illustration shows an excellent early nineteenth-century one. Most characteristic are the various treatments of outside steps made necessary by the steep grades met with everywhere.

The interiors of these alluring houses are fully as interesting as the exteriors. No good American should fail to see the truly exquisite rooms and the wonderful staircase of the Lee Mansion, which is without a peer in this country. Nor should he fail to see the King Hooper house, to appreciate the wholesome beauty of the second-period panelling and fireplaces of this fine example.

There are other buildings in town of special interest—the old Town House, the Powder House of 1750, and the old North Church, each worthy of a visit, as is the burial-ground, to remind us of the frailty of us humans and of the fact that our forefathers used to make better lettering than we do.

By all means, gentle reader, visit Marblehead, and you will profit greatly thereby; spend at least a day if a layman, and at least a week if you are an architect. Read up in Mr. Road's History the stories of Mugford the brave sailor who captured the British transport "Hope" when in command of the American schooner

Entrance Porch.
HOUSE ON WASHINGTON STREET, MARBLEHEAD,
MASSACHUSETTS.

Doorway.
GENERAL JOHN GLOVER HOUSE, MARBLEHEAD,
MASSACHUSETTS.
Built in 1762. The home of the famous Revolutionary general.

"Franklin," of Agnes Surriage and Sir John Frankland, of Gerry and Storey, of the gallant General Glover and his regiment, whose soldiers, according to tradition, rowed Washington across the Delaware River on that famous wintry night, December 25th, 1776. Read the real story of Skipper Ireson, that much maligned seaman, whom Whittier immortalized in the same poem in which the women of Marblehead are unjustly given the rôle of avenging furies. Poor Ireson! He was given the ride on the rail in the tarry and feathery coat, but not by the women of Marblehead. The perpetrators of this outrage were fishermen of the town whose indignation had been aroused by the stories of the crew of Ireson's schooner, who had forced him against his will to abandon the other craft in distress. Ireson's crew were at fault and shifted the blame to their skipper when the story came out. Learn how completely American a Massachusetts town has been and always will be. Just imagine—the curfew tolls every evening at nine and the boys and girls celebrate Guy Fawkes day every November fifth with bonfires and a procession!

Entrance Porch.
THE COL. WILLIAM R. LEE MANSION,
MARBLEHEAD, MASSACHUSETTS.
Like the Col. Jeremiah Lee Mansion, this house is also surmounted by a cupola. The parlor was elaborately decorated by an Italian artist.

HOUSE IN LOOKOUT COURT,
MARBLEHEAD, MASSACHUSETTS.

The elliptical fan-light and reeded pilasters give to this very old house a distinct architectural character.

Marblehead, Part II

THE ORIGINAL settlement of Salem included within its area land now divided between Beverly, Peabody, Wenham, Manchester, Danvers, and Marblehead. It also covered Middleton, and parts of Topsfield and Essex. Marblehead itself was settled about 1629, although there exists a local tradition that its first resident was a man named Doliber, who came from the original group occupying Salem—then known as "Naumkeag"—previous to the arrival of Capt. John Endecott in June of 1628.

This legend extends into certain ramifying details that establish the site of his occupancy as one of the coves on or near Peach's Point,—and the form of his original residence as a fish hogshead!

Whether this be fact or fable, this convenient harbor was immediately appreciated by these early fisher-folk,—and by 1629, at least, it had begun to develop as a fishing village, at first called "Nanepashemet"—from the chief of the Naumkeag tribe of Indians who were found residing in the Salem area by the first English settlers. History—or, it still may be, legend—persists in claiming the original inhabitants who settled these rocky headlands, as fishermen from the islands of Guernsey and Jersey, in the British Channel, just off the coast of France.

The first "Meeting House" was located on the top of the steep, rocky elevation known as "Old Burying Hill"; still one of the highest sites in the town, with a number of protected coves lying near its base, and "Beacon Hill" just beyond. The picturesque little section of "Barnegat," with its pebbled beach crowded with fishing shacks, lobster pots, drying nets, and floats, and drawn-up dories nearby—still remains as a picture of the life that probably then—and for a hundred years and more thereafter—abounded in the little coves about the original church site, where the first Meeting House may have been built as early as 1638. From the "Burying Hill" you can still look down upon the placid landlocked waters of "Little Harbor"—with "Gerry's Island" only a few yards off shore,—reached over a sand bar at low tide—where the first minister of the town, Parson William Walton dwelt from 1638 to 1668.

On one of the headlands of "Peach's Point" adjoining, stood the "Mr. Craddock's House" of which Winthrop wrote in his Journal, in September of 1633, "Mr. Craddock's House at Marblehead was burned down at midnight before, there being in it Mr. Allerton and many fishermen whom he employed that season, who were all preserved by a special providence of God, with most of his goods there, by a tailor, who sat up that night at work in the house, and hearing a noise, looked out and saw the house on fire above the oven in the thatch." This was the Isaac Allerton of Plymouth Colony, who was probably in Marblehead as early as 1629,—and may have been carrying on his enterprises in partnership with Craddock, who was the first London governor of the Massachusetts Company and was actively engaged in the fishing business.

From Marblehead was launched the third vessel built in the Colony, called the "Desire," which returned from one of her early voyages to the West Indies, with the first cargo of slaves introduced into New England. Marblehead was named a "plantation" in 1635, and set apart from Salem in 1649; being incorporated by act of the General Court on May 2nd of that year.

The town originally grew up about the occasional fishermen's shacks, scattered irregularly upon the infrequent levels of the cliffs along the harbor, or clustered upon the few beaches to be found here and there at their base.

There could obviously not have been much order or regularity in such a Topsy-like growth as must have followed along this irregular shore. The first shacks were gradually replaced with small houses of two or three rooms, set any-which-way, wherever a small bit of level ground could be found, beside the paths that meandered up and down the rocky hillsides. Later, streets roughly paralleling the harbor line developed

VIEW ALONG HOOPER STREET, LOOKING WEST
THE "KING" HOOPER MANSION — 1745 — MARBLEHEAD, MASSACHUSETTS

precariously; "Front," backed again by "Washington" Street; with only one fairly level and straight street connecting them; "State," leading from the "Town Landing" up to the old "Town Square."

As, gradually, the old paths climbing the bluffs were superseded, wherever it was possible (though many still remain!) by wider twisting but still tortuously narrow ways; the little houses were partly turned about, had new rooms and fronts added, or—as was the case with the "King" Hooper building—an entirely new portion was built in 1745 to face the street,

the identical old site where first it took root. But Marblehead, dour in the stubbornness and content in the ignorance of its "98 per cent American ancestry," has thrown away no less than *three* opportunities to preserve its old picturesqueness! Its first settlement, about Fort Sewall and Little Harbor, had moved southwestward by 1700 to 1750 to a newer "Town Square" a full half mile; and this was, by a hundred and fifty years later, again abandoned for the still newer business center now at Washington and Atlantic Avenue,—but its too canny inhabitants, over three

OLD "TOWN SQUARE," MARBLEHEAD, MASSACHUSETTS

PHOTOGRAPH TAKEN IN 1926 BEFORE THE REMOVAL OF WATERS HOUSE AND BAKERY (1683) AT THE LEFT

against one end of the older gambrel house that still backs it. In the case of the Capt. Samuel Trevett house, this was crowded in on the north-eastern side of wandering Washington Street, well out upon the roadway, with its back against the higher rocky bluff, upon which a small doorway opens from the lower terrace of a crowding garden, from the upper levels of which one can almost see the harbor over the house!

It is not often a New England town is given three chances to retain its original identity, undisturbed— as usually it has to reproduce its integral parts upon

hundred years, have lacked entirely the business acumen and common-sense to conserve its greatest asset and charm, the individual and historic character of its old-time glamour,—that might have been kept for all time, with no interruption in its business development and modern growth,—which still continues, faster and ranker, to the south and west!

But, besides the old "Town Square," here shown, with its wooden Town House of 1727, as it appeared before the left hand group of buildings was demolished in 1937; it is still possible to find—here and there—an

Entrance Detail
THE OLD TOWN HALL—1727—"TOWN SQUARE," MARBLEHEAD, MASSACHUSETTS

LEE STREET, LOOKING EAST
MARBLEHEAD, MASSACHUSETTS

old street or a cluster of buildings; a weathered Fish house or Fisherman's Cottage; old Boat Shop, or remaining Boat Yard. But they all are passing fast. With the construction of a new sewer, some five and six years ago, there vanished almost instantly a whole flock of privies, that had for generations perched here and there, higglety-pigglety, about the back and side yards of the town, at all heights and angles—wherever a promising declivity or rock fissure could be found! And with them vanished no small part of the old-town atmosphere,—though here and there about the harbor there remain evanescent flavors of the old fish flakes and dressing grounds to attract the gulls—and cats!— as well as the visiting firemen and rich westerners in search of historic cultural American backgrounds!

In many old house interiors, where the paneled fireplace ends show sloping ceilings to the side walls, there has been a belief that they were originally built in that manner to simulate the curving lines of ship-cabins. This may actually have been occasionally the case; but it nevertheless is the fact that this type of interior appearance is not confined exclusively to the coast, as rooms of this character are often found on sites located at considerable distances from the ocean. It is, further, undoubtedly the fact, that many of these effects are accidental, while the floors have sub-

sided, the chimney and hearth have been kept up by their masonry support, so that the hearth slopes off from the underfire, along with the floor; or the under-fire or hearth remains raised, often some inches above the floor level at sides and front, where floor slopes away from it, and down toward the two side walls.

In the Hooper house north west second floor front bedroom, this effect appears—but the difference in level can hardly be over one and a half to two inches, and the floor slopes as well from the hearth to both sides, and from the fireplace wall toward the front of the room. In the other chamber it is more marked, the difference being at least three to four inches, but again it appears on both the floor and ceiling of this room, though it is not apparent upon the floor above.

In the Trevett House, these differences are still more marked. In both upper front rooms, the slopes show in the ceiling, more in the room on the eastern than the western side of the hall—but in both cases there exists evidence of the floor having had a similar unevenness at least partially corrected—showing in the bases beside the hearth in the eastern room, and in a raised underfire and hearth in the room across the hall.

In the first floor west side room there is a 14 inch soffit under the beam forming part of the

GLOVER COURT, LOOKING NORTH
MARBLEHEAD, MASSACHUSETTS

OLD HOUSES OFF THE ROAD TO FORT SEWALL, MARBLEHEAD, MASSACHUSETTS

cornice back to the face of the fireplace paneling, its soffit slopes upward at least two to two and a half inches, including the warped mouldings of the bed-moulding, while in the east room a still wider plaster soffit, from its front edge, warps up at the center to meet the higher fireplace paneling at this point.

ceilings seem to be brought at the front—or opposite —walls of the rooms, to a nearly level line,—which persists along the major part of the side walls, as well. In other words, so far as these two houses provide examples of so-called "Ship Rooms," in a distinctly seafaring community, there exists evidence to show that

WASHINGTON STREET ELEVATION

CAPT. SAMUEL TREVETT HOUSE—BEFORE 1750—MARBLEHEAD, MASSACHUSETTS

But in the room at the back the beam crossing in front of the second floor hearth, while straight, exposes behind it, the under part of the arch of the second floor hearth, from each side of which the ceiling slopes sharply to the side walls, where it is lower by almost five inches! In all these rooms the plaster

these inequalities occurred through settlement or shrinkage of wood supports in contrast to the portion of the walls supported by the masonry of the chimney construction. Which does not disprove that there may still exist "Ship Rooms," intentionally so finished, far from the tang and roar of the ocean!

OLD HOUSES ON WASHINGTON STREET, LOOKING SOUTH-EAST FROM TRAINING FIELD, MARBLEHEAD, MASSACHUSETTS

OLD HOUSES ON FRANKLIN STREET, LOOKING NORTH-EAST
MARBLEHEAD, MASSACHUSETTS

66

SOUTH ELEVATION—OLDER REAR PORTION
THE "KING" HOOPER MANSION, MARBLEHEAD, MASSACHUSETTS

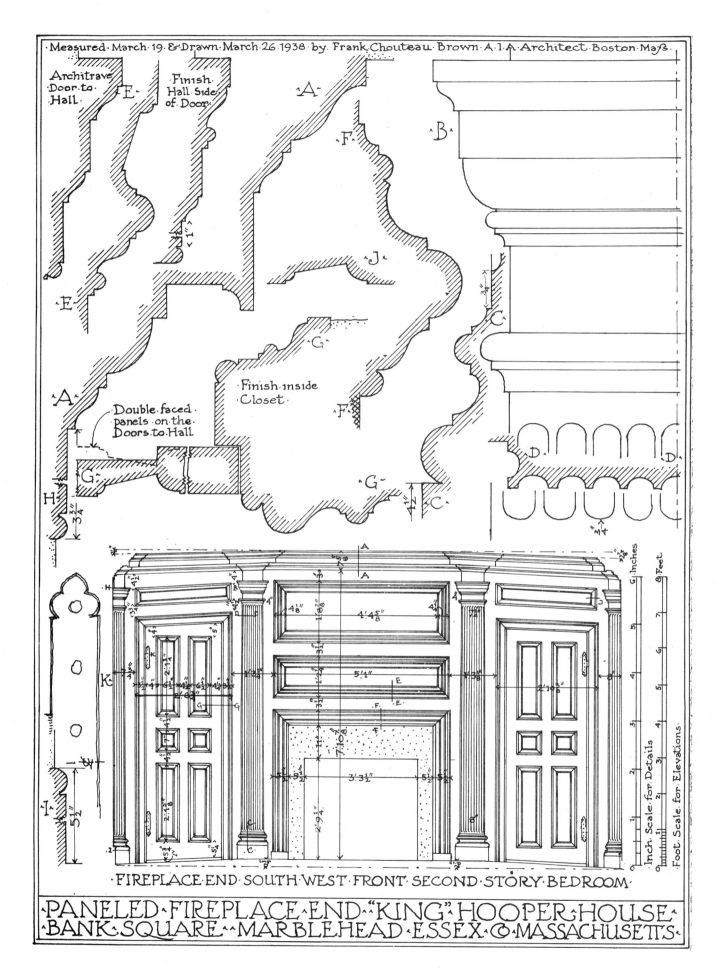

Architrave
Door to
Hall

Finish
Hall Side
of Door

·E·

·A·

·B·

·F·

·J·

·E·

·C·

·A·

Double faced
panels on the
Doors to Hall

Finish inside
Closet

·G·

·F·

·G·

·D·

·D·

·H·

·G·

·G·

·C·

·K·

FIREPLACE·END·SOUTH·WEST·FRONT·SECOND·STORY·BEDROOM·

G·Inches

8·Feet

·Inch·Scale·for·Details·

·Foot·Scale·for·Elevations·

PANELED·FIREPLACE·END·"KING"·HOOPER·HOUSE·
·BANK·SQUARE·MARBLEHEAD·ESSEX·CO·MASSACHUSETTS·

VIEW OF HALL FROM FIRST FLOOR—NORTH-WEST FRONT ROOM
THE "KING" HOOPER MANSION—1745—MARBLEHEAD, MASSACHUSETTS

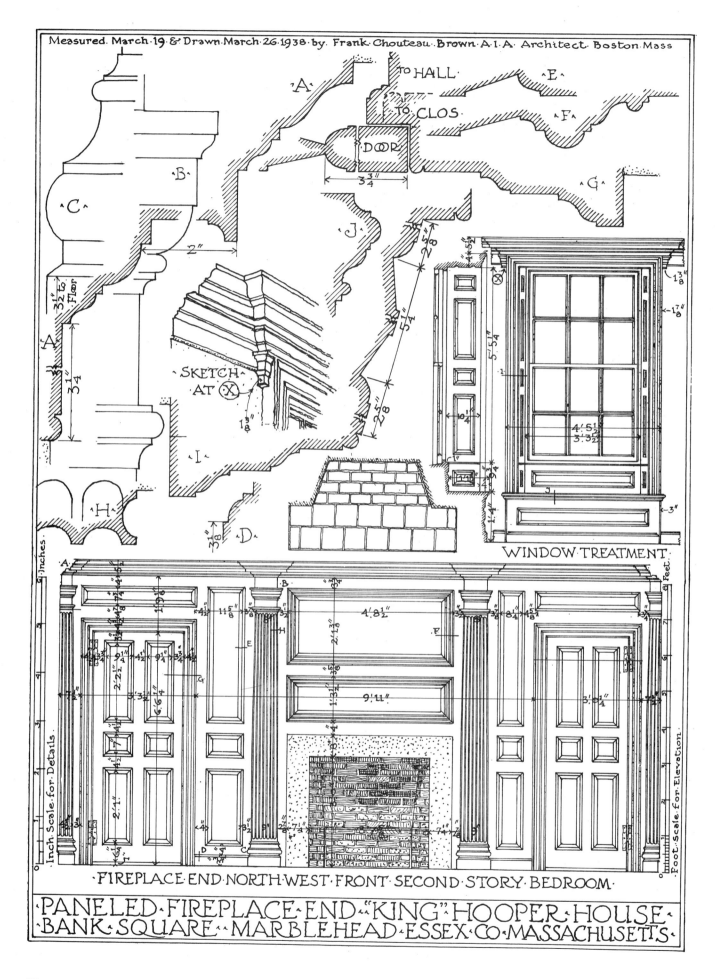

Measured. March. 19. & Drawn. March. 26. 1938 by. Frank. Chouteau. Brown. A.I.A. Architect. Boston. Mass

·A·

TO HALL

·E·

·F·

TO CLOS

·B·

DOOR

·G·

·C·

3¾″

·J·

SKETCH
AT ⊗

SKETCH AT ⊗

WINDOW·TREATMENT

·I·

·H·

·D·

FIREPLACE·END·NORTH·WEST·FRONT·SECOND·STORY·BEDROOM·

PANELED·FIREPLACE·END·"KING"·HOOPER·HOUSE·
BANK·SQUARE·MARBLEHEAD·ESSEX·CO·MASSACHUSETTS·

70

FIREPLACE END—NORTH-WEST SECOND STORY FRONT BEDROOM

FIREPLACE END—SOUTH-WEST SECOND STORY FRONT BEDROOM
THE "KING" HOOPER MANSION—1745—MARBLEHEAD, MASSACHUSETTS

First Floor—Northeast Rear Room
THE CAPT. SAMUEL TREVETT HOUSE—BEFORE 1750—WASHINGTON STREET, MARBLEHEAD

First Floor—East Front Room

First Floor—West Front Room

THE CAPT. SAMUEL TREVETT HOUSE—BEFORE 1750—MARBLEHEAD, MASSACHUSETTS

Detail of Facade—"New Portion" (c. 1780)
COL. WILLIAM R. LEE HOUSE—1745—MARBLEHEAD, MASSACHUSETTS

Marblehead, Part III

ALTHOUGH the fine shelter provided by the "Little Harbor" at Marblehead (the larger anchorage lies open to gales from the North-East) was appreciated from the beginning by the fisherfolk from the English Channel Islands who were its first settlers; yet, despite their occasional increase by newcomers, probably from Lincolnshire, the growth of this portion of the Salem settlement seems to have been very slow. A nineteen year old graduate of Harvard college— Mr. John Cotton, a grandson of Cotton Mather— coming to teach at Marblehead about 1698, wrote in a letter of six years later, "When I came to this place —the whole township was not much bigger than a large farm, and very rocky, and so they are forc't to get their living out of the sea, not having room to confound the fisherman with the husbandman, and so spoil both as they do in some places. It has a very good Harbour which they improve to the best advantage for Fishing both Summer and Winter - - - And finally it is one of the best country places to keep school in, providing a man be firmly fix't in principles of virtue and religion, which I heartily wish were more abundant among them in the life and power of it."

There are various stories as to the derivation of the name of Marblehead. A quotation from a letter of the Rev. Francis Higgenson, written in 1629, is often given as its basis. He wrote, "here is plentie of marble-stone in such store that we have great rocks of it and a harbour nearby; our plantation is from thence called 'Marble Harbour' "—a name that shortly after appeared changed to Marblehead, possibly because of the number of adjoining headlands locally termed 'Heads'—such as 'Goodwin's Head,' 'Naugus Head.'

After the death of the first Minister, Parson William Walton, in 1668, Mr. Samuel Cheever, an Harvard graduate was appointed, at 80 pounds the year (much of which he had to accept in merchandise— probably largely of fish!—on account of shortage of currency). This is known because of an existing town record, "resolved that 70% of Mr. Cheever's salary should be paid in cash. Those refusing to pay in coin to have 25% added to their tax which is to be paid in good merchandise, the value thereof fixed by two impartial persons."

He was succeeded by Parson John Barnard in 1716, who continued till his death in 1770. He refused the presidency of Harvard in 1737, which was then accepted by Edward Holyoke of the Second Congregational Church—also of Marblehead. Meanwhile, St. Michael's (the oldest church building in New England) was built in 1714, cruciform in plan, and with frame and materials sent from England. It still retains its ancient reredos, with credo and decalogue, black with age,—although the original plan has been rather obscured by an addition added across one end. The Rev. David Mossom, its second rector, afterward removed to Virginia, where he married George Washington and Martha Custis.

Beside St. Michael's, the oldest church building now existing in Marblehead is the structure known as "The Old North," on Washington Street, not far from the Old Town House, in the Square, and just beyond the Capt. Trevett House. This is the third edifice of the First Congregational Church, and dates from 1824. It has a granite facade, with an interesting tower or belfry, with a part of the sounding board from the second church pulpit, and an old fish weathervane now on the tower, which was also taken from the second building, built in 1695. Of the original structure of the "First Church," or Meeting House, there have been preserved several portions of the panelled fronts and doors of the old Oaken Pews, taken from this original building of 1648—which have never been painted, with the exception of the oval back of the pew number. While the mouldings and styles differ somewhat, yet they all exhibit a fine precision of workmanship,—and are perhaps the oldest bits of ecclesiastical architectural detail remaining in New England. The original pulpit of the third edifice, of rosewood, is in use in the present building.

It happens that we have another word picture of

75

Marblehead; that given by Mr. Barnard, also when he arrived in the town, in November of 1715. He wrote, "There were two companies of poor, smoke dried, rude, ill clothed men without military discipline. There was not one proper carpenter, mason, tailor, nor butcher in the town nor any market worth naming. They had their houses built by country workmen, their clothes made out of town and supplied themselves with beef and pork from Boston, which

this time still exhibit,—though it is to be remembered that it was during his ministry that the men were encouraged to take their own ships farther afield; and so secure to themselves the profits from their work, and bring back the much needed cash in exchange. It was from these ventures, finally, that the first merchant fortunes of the town were derived.

One of the most famous residents among the many who came from Marblehead, was the Col. John

COL. WILLIAM R. LEE HOUSE—1745—WASHINGTON STREET, MARBLEHEAD

drained the town of its money. Nor was there a foreign trading vessel belonging to the town. The people left the merchants of Boston, Salem, and Europe to carry away the gains by which means the town was always dismally poor and as rude, swearing, drunken and fighting a crew as they were poor."

It seems the more remarkable that from such rude surroundings should arise such fine dwellings—and especially so many early dwellings of three story height—as the early houses that have come down to

Glover, of the Fourteenth Continentals, of Revolutionary fame, who headed the "Amphibious Regiment" of Marbleheaders whose knowledge of the sea, and its tricks, made possibly two of the most famous exploits of Washington's army; and may have been instrumental in winning the war of Independence. These were, of course, the secret ferrying across the river from Long Island of the entire American army of 9000 men, with horses, cannon and supplies, in one foggy night, of thirteen hours; and the equally impossible

The Stair Hall
COL. WILLIAM R. LEE HOUSE—1745—MARBLEHEAD, MASSACHUSETTS

feat of crossing the Delaware in a winter storm on Christmas Day and surprising the Hessians, secure in their winter quarters at Trenton, outside Philadelphia.

John Glover was born in Salem, November 5, 1732. With his three brothers, he came to Marblehead; worked as shoemaker, fisherman, merchant, and served in the militia, becoming a captain in 1773. He ended the War as a Brigadier-General, and served on the Court-Martial that tried Maj. Andre.

Other famous Marbleheaders would include Commodore Samuel Tucker, Col. Azor Orne, Capt. John Selman, Gov. Elbridge Gerry, Maj. John Pedrick, Judge Joseph Story, Chief-Justice Sewell, and Peter Jayne. Two more, who belong almost to the legendary group, would be Skipper Ireson of Whittier's poem and Agnes Surriage, who in later years married Sir Harry Frankland, whom she met when he—as Collector of the Port of Boston—was often in Marblehead while superintending the construction of Fort Sewall, at the entrance to the Harbor, in 1742.

Of the several old Lee family houses in Marblehead, the "Lee Mansion," was built in 1768 by Jeremiah Lee, who died in 1775; and while the one perhaps best known to visitors from being the home of the Marblehead Historical Society, and well filled with its treasures,—yet the home of Colonel William R. Lee, which was earlier known as "The House on the Hill" for thirty years or so before the Mansion was built, is one of the most notable of the older landmarks of the town. Placed looking south over the old Training Field, it was originally a narrow two-room-to-the-floor, three-story dwelling, with its end to the street;

WALL PAPER IN THE DRAWING ROOM
COL. WILLIAM R. LEE HOUSE—1745—MARBLEHEAD, MASSACHUSETTS

it may have been the house that was mentioned as being upon this site still twenty years earlier in 1725.

The house was built by Col. Lee's grandfather, Samuel Lee, and originally faced south-west,—while parts of the old stairway and Hall, with the old front door, are still to be seen in their proper locations in the old building. But shortly after Jeremiah—who was the Uncle of Col. Wm. R. Lee—built his Mansion House further down the street, Col. Lee—who had

ous newel and unusual baluster spacing that appears in the photographs. The new room at the south-east corner was given a new chimney and end treatment, with deep arched recesses, and the larger room across the hall was furnished, a few years later, with the gorgeous and unique oriental scenery paper known as "The Pilgrimage of Omar" showing a view of the Bosphorous and old Stamboul, which still retains all its striking colorfulness. It was probably made about

WALL PAPER IN THE DRAWING ROOM
COL. WILLIAM R. LEE HOUSE—1745—MARBLEHEAD, MASSACHUSETTS

formed the local artillery company—took off the easternmost room of the old House and built the "new front" facing south-east upon the street, and the old "Training Field"; raising the story heights, and taking the older carved balusters of the lower flight of the old stairway to use them over again in the new stairway and Hall of the front part of the building. The "new stairway" was built about 1790, shortly after the front portion was occupied; and has the curi-

1800—perhaps by Defour—and is not duplicated elsewhere in New England.

The Lee family originally came from Manchester, Massachusetts; and it was Justice Samuel L. Lee (1667-1754) who was also known as a builder and owner of numerous pieces of property,—as well as for being the father of thirteen children—who built the house now best known as the Colonel William Raymond Lee Dwelling. When the latter altered it, and added the new three story front sometime about 1780 to 1790, he greatly increased the story heights, making the new first floor 9' 5" high where the old one was only 7' 6", and so occasioning many interesting—and unexpected!—differences of level in going from one portion of the house to another, as well as requiring several short flights of stairs;—the last of which leads up to the level of the Banquet Room, which ran the entire width of the new front upon the upper story, between fireplaces of the same design placed at both ends.

The "Lee Mansion" below the Hill, and nearly across "Bank Square" from the "King" Hooper House, is one of the most-visited dwellings in New England. Even the Kitchen has a magnificent paneled end, over a fireplace that is six feet long and four and a half feet high. This Kitchen, by the way, opened at the rear, into an old passage that led to the Slaves Quarters and Cookhouse,—a lower brick two-story building, still existing, at the right of the main house, then providing shelter for the coach on the lower floor.

Not the least detail of interest in this fine old dwelling is the Side Stairway, that runs from the fine entrance on the Northeast end, up to the third story, while the same baluster and post design continues from the middle of that floor up into the roof Cupola. This stairway has an unusual, yet simple and practical, treatment of the wall dado, that has particular architectural interest. It should be noted that the main staircase does not continue above the second floor hall; the upper floor being reached only by this Side stairway, or by means of a so-called "secret" stairway, off a closet beside the chimney between the bedrooms at the opposite end of the building.

These two principal front bedrooms are beautiful and spacious interiors, though the mantel pieces are much simpler than on the floor below, having only the large panels extending to the ceiling to mark their importance, compared to the pilasters framing the Parlour fire-opening in the room at the right; and the fine and high relief carving, after the English manner, that ornaments the Banquet Room fireplace. In design and treatment the latter much resembles the carved oak mantel in the "Bishop's Palace" in Cambridge, Massachusetts,—although the work is here executed in pine, which is now grained, although originally believed to have been painted white.

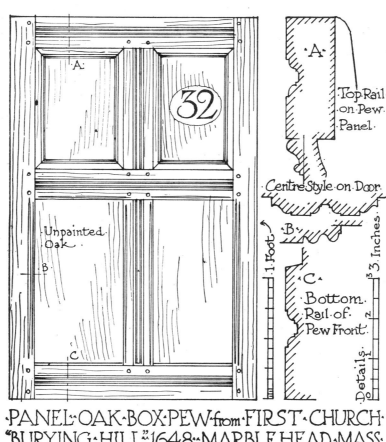

·PANEL·OAK·BOX·PEW·from·FIRST·CHURCH· "BURYING·HILL"·1648·MARBLEHEAD·MASS·

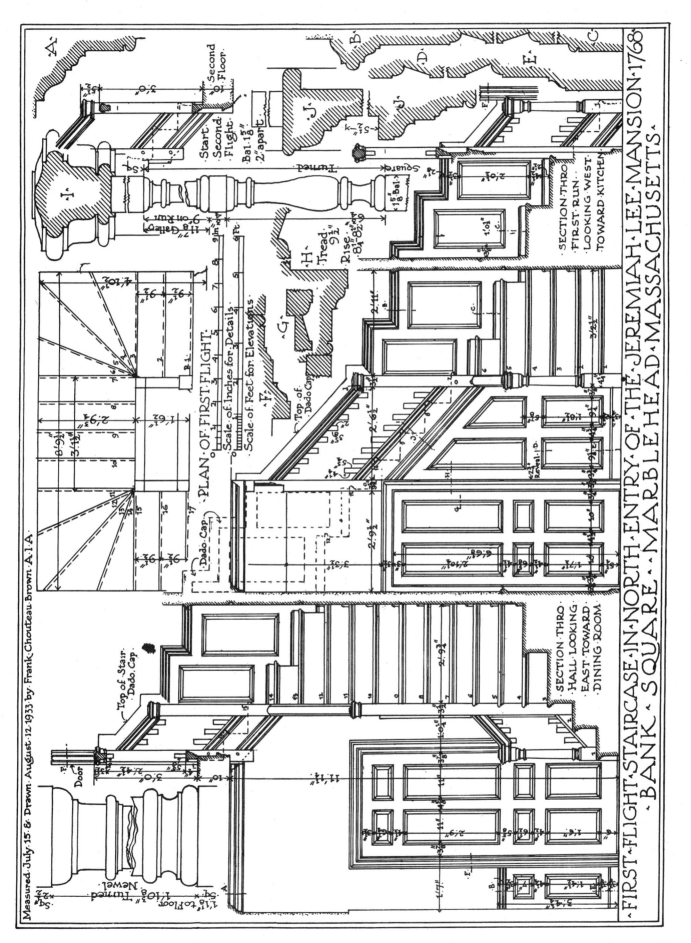

FIRST·FLIGHT·STAIRCASE·IN·NORTH·ENTRY·OF·THE·JEREMIAH·LEE·MANSION·1768·
·BANK·SQUARE··MARBLEHEAD·MASSACHUSETTS·

Measured·July·15·&·Drawn·August·12·1933·by·Frank·Chouteau·Brown·A.I.A.

PLAN·OF·FIRST·FLIGHT·

SECTION·THRO·
FIRST·RUN·
LOOKING·WEST·
TOWARD·KITCHEN·

SECTION·THRO·
HALL·LOOKING·
EAST·TOWARD·
DINING·ROOM·

FIREPLACE END IN "NEW PORTION" (ABOUT 1780)

THE COL. WILLIAM R. LEE HOUSE—1745—WASHINGTON STREET, MARBLEHEAD, MASSACHUSETTS

OLD STAIRCASE, REAR OF SECOND FLOOR   STAIRCASE FROM FIRST TO SECOND FLOOR

THE COL. WILLIAM R. LEE HOUSE—1745—WASHINGTON STREET, MARBLEHEAD, MASSACHUSETTS

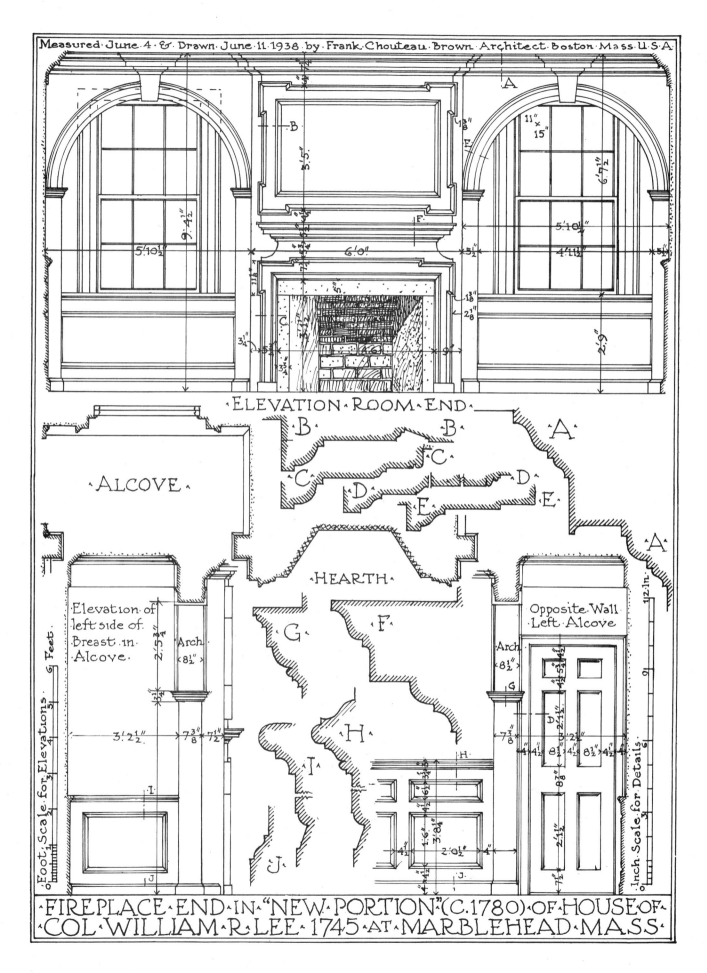

Measured June 4 & Drawn June 11 1938 by Frank Chouteau Brown Architect Boston Mass U.S.A.

· ELEVATION · ROOM · END ·

· ALCOVE ·

· HEARTH ·

Elevation of
left side of
Breast in
Alcove.

Opposite Wall
Left Alcove

· FIREPLACE · END · IN · "NEW · PORTION" · (C·1780) · OF · HOUSE · OF ·
· COL · WILLIAM · R · LEE · 1745 · AT · MARBLEHEAD · MASS ·

THE DRAWING ROOM

SOUTH EAST ROOM—SECOND FLOOR

COL. WILLIAM R. LEE HOUSE—1745—MARBLEHEAD, MASSACHUSETTS

THE OLDEST EPISCOPAL CHURCH IN NEW ENGLAND
ST. MICHAEL'S CHURCH—1714—MARBLEHEAD, MASSACHUSETTS

OLD NORTH CHURCH—1824—MARBLEHEAD, MASSACHUSETTS

CAPT. ASA HOOPER HOUSE, 5 WASHINGTON ST., MARBLEHEAD, MASS.

Marblehead, Part IV

THE early growth of the town was not very rapid. By 1674 the Town records had listed 114 householders; while in Town meeting that same year it was voted that "all these fifteen or sixteen houses built in Marblehead before ye year 1660, shall be allowed one cowes common and a halfe." Most of the "Commons" set apart as public land owned in common by the community in the earlier settled townships of New England were intended either for grazing land, for the use of the cattle of the townspeople, or as a "training field" for the regular meetings of its "train band," the first colonial militia.

Besides its "Training Field," the town early allotted "the Neck" for general use as "Cow Commons." The "Neck" was a rocky peninsula, almost entirely detached from the mainland, except at low tide, when a shallow sand bar from its westernmost end formed the inner limits of the large harbor. A slight obstruction across this natural causeway kept the cattle confined to the grazing area, even at low water. It was this same Neck—which was practically an island at high tide—that gave protection to the larger anchorage that is now known as "the Harbor,"—although in the first hundred years of its settlement, the fishermen and small vessels using the town facilities took advantage of the better protected "Little Harbor," a small bay just back of the promontory crowned by Fort Sewall, at the very foot of "Burying Hill," which was the site of the first settlement.

The importance of this harbor to the early settlement would be indicated by the several forts that were erected for its protection and defence at various times. Most important of these is Fort Sewall, built on the mainland side of the harbor entrance. This position was first fortified in very early times. During King Philip's war, which began in 1675 and continued for three years, this fort and its three large cannon were placed in order, and it has been continued and improved from time to time up nearly to the present day. The structure now to be seen dates from about 1742,

when it was enlarged and reconstructed under Sir Harry Frankland. This position was garrisoned in three important wars and, although again somewhat rebuilt and remodelled in 1864, it still retains the older magazine, along with several old gun emplacements and other features.

Another old fort, known as Fort Washington, was constructed and in use during the Revolution and the War of 1812, on the high rocky bluff overlooking Orne Street, from near the "Old Burying Hill," although, along with an embankment that at one time dominated the causeway, at the southern end of the main harbor, it has long since disappeared. One other earthwork fortification could, until within the last dozen years, be plainly traced at Naugus Head—the tip of the Cape nearest Salem Harbor. The dirt roadway around that headland that served a group of summer cottages cut right through the embankment in two places, and its main outlines were still easily traced, despite the location of some of the houses across and upon its outer slopes.

Along with this group might be mentioned the old "Powder House," a fine example of the town magazine of the time, that was built by vote of the town, in 1755, at the outbreak of the French and Indian War, and continued in use through the Revolution and the War of 1812. It is a handsome example of brickwork, laid in Flemish bond, circular in plan and with a brick-domed top, covered by its "ogee" shingled roof, located on what used to be known as "the Ferry Road." It is about the earliest and best example of a building of this type remaining within the Commonwealth; although the "Gun House," built to house the artillery of the local regiment during the War of 1812, is probably more unique. In its simplicity this unusual building might almost suggest a post-Colonial precedent for the modern garage, if to be built of brick! The principal walls are again laid in an early bond.

This records an unusual number of public buildings, of both age and historic association, still preserved in one small township,—except that no specific mention

ROBIE HOUSE—1729—7 PEARL STREET, MARBLEHEAD, MASSACHUSETTS

has yet been made of the Town House built in 1727 exclusively for that purpose and continued in use until 1877, when Abbot Hall, an ugly brick structure of Victorian type, was built on the old "Training Field" and given to the townspeople for a meeting place. The old Town House formerly had a Market under it on the ground floor level—as was so commonly the case in many sections of old England—which also explains its high basement.

a successful economic solution for his pastorate from those conditions amongst which he had found them than upon his eminence as a spiritual leader. For Marblehead—in common with most other smaller townships—was then desperately contending for its prosperity and future livelihood against capitalistic control, in the first instance imposed by its English sponsors, but later furthered both by the governmental and merchandising functions common to the

THE AZOR ORNE HOUSE, ORNE STREET, MARBLEHEAD, MASSACHUSETTS

If we glance back over the early records of the colonies, it will be realized that there must have been more than a merely spiritual reason for all the early settlement groups to have so continually evolved about their preacher's leadership. He must have possessed temporal as well as spiritual power to have been able to lead his flock successfully into this new world wilderness, and bring them to a permanent fruition. And so it would seem that the high repute attained by Parson John Barnard in this community was based rather upon his business acumen in finding

period. So long as the residents of this little fishing community were content to remain an adjunct to the larger and more prosperous trading port of nearby Salem; so long as they were content to endure the privations inherent in the fisherman's calling, and allow the merchants of Salem to carry their product to the larger cities where it was most in demand, they must also expect them to obtain the major part of the profits. And the more especially when they were accustomed to accept, locally, other merchandise in exchange for their fish; while these middlemen mer-

THE ORNE HOUSE, ORNE STREET, MARBLEHEAD, MASSACHUSETTS

chants took to themselves not only the ample benefits of coined currency payments for the fish, but also exacted metal money payment for the costs of its carriage to market!

And it was this problem that Parson Barnard solved by persuading the Marbleheaders to convey their own fish to market, and so themselves profit both from the savings made in its transport and the currency payments. It was shortly after this that the town entered upon its new prosperity and period of more preten-

in the classical fashion of the time, that extend over the walls of the two-storied main hall, and the two principal rooms upon the second floor. Obviously, all of the panels originally must have been painted to fit the spaces between doors and window trim, and extending from dado cap to cornice facia.

The Jeremiah Lee Mansion is, perhaps, almost the best New England example of that type of "Colonial" architecture that might be most correctly termed "Georgian,"—a word much misused! In old England

FIREPLACE AND PANELING SECOND FLOOR
JEREMIAH LEE MANSION—1768—MARBLEHEAD, MASSACHUSETTS

tious building. And, at once, some of the new three story dwellings—including probably the Robie house, of brick, built about 1729—began to demonstrate this new influx of wealth. And from then on, as in the other houses already illustrated, did the architecture of the town express the change in its manners of living, culminating finally in the Lee Mansion, of 1768.

Some further evidence of its dignified detail, furnishing, and decoration appears on these pages, including particularly the fine mantels, and the unusual painted wall coverings executed in gray monotone and white,

it usually refers to a structure of similar design, but generally built of either brick or stone. In America, brick was also used generally for dwellings of this kind in the South, but in the New England colonies—where wood was always the favored material—it was sometimes, as in this present instance, employed so as to suggest, or rather to simulate, the formal stone coursing of England—as in the regions around Bath—for a dwelling of this pretentious kind.

So the use of wooden boards, with both horizontal and perpendicular grooves, disposed to suggest the jointing of a masonry wall, was not an uncommon treatment for important dwellings in towns along the coast. In some cases it was employed upon the front alone. In other instances it was used upon the front and two ends; and sometimes—although more rarely —on all four sides of the structure. In Marblehead, both the Lee houses—as well as the "King" Hooper house—have shown this use of wood as an outer wall covering. So, too, did the "Lindens," formerly in Danvers; and it is also occasionally found on dwellings in Salem, Hingham, Newburyport, Portsmouth, Portland, Providence, and other cities and towns in New England. It is an even more common treatment to find wooden "quoins" used on the corners of old Colonial wooden buildings in place of the simpler upright corner board.

Another feature employed in common by the two Lee Houses, is the "Cupola" on the center of the roof ridge,—that, in the more dignified and formally designed coast dwelling, sometimes supplants the simpler "Captain's walk," that was built over the roofs of many old houses along the coast, at the old harbors of the mainland and, especially, in great numbers, in such a sea faring island port as Nantucket. Their chief reason for being was to give the occupants of these houses easy access to the roof to overlook and keep track of the shipping in the harbor and the boats that entered and left its anchorage on their many voyages from the port.

Both Jeremiah Lee and Col. Azor Orne were elected to the Continental Congress, as well as being members of the province "Committee of Safety and Supplies," and the two, along with their fellow-townsman, Elbridge Gerry (afterwards vice-president of the United States), were very nearly surprised at Cambridge by the British soldiers, on the night of April 18, 1775, when they had remained in the Black Horse Tavern after a later meeting of the province committee, escaping at the very last moment, with only a few clothes, —of the result of which exposure Mr. Lee died just three weeks later.

The Azor Orne house is another Marblehead example of the three story town house—although, rather unusually, with gable ends; and a late doorway—of which, however, the rear view shown here is more locally characteristic; indicating, as it does, the way the houses in that town are sometimes located against the base of the rocky bluffs that often crowd upon and overlook their narrow backyards. This dwelling is situated on the street of the same name, off the turn at the end of Washington Street into Franklin, facing out toward the harbor. The home of Parson Barnard is on Franklin Street, just around the corner; a large gambrel roof dwelling, enshrouded in fine old trees, of nice proportions, but with little authentic detail remaining from its many changes and repairs.

Inside its later Greek doorway, the Orne house has a fine stairway of the period of about 1770, with fireplaces and cornices quite similar to those of the simpler types to be found in the Lee Mansion; along with the rooms with simple paneled end, of which two examples are shown herewith.

But, after all, the distinctive charm of Marblehead does not reside in its more pretentious dwellings, handsome and much visited as they are; but rather in the more informal and picturesque groupings of old weatherworn sided structures, placed at all possible angles to the street, and to their neighbors, in which certain sections of the old town still abound. While, to a lesser extent, at Newcastle and upon some portions of the "old River Road" along the Merrimac in Amesbury, and at one or two sections of Portsmouth, and a few bits around the harbor at Gloucester, a few similar glimpses may now be seen—and, to an even greater extent, they will probably continue and be preserved on the island at Nantucket—certainly nowhere else so near to Boston may so much of the charm of an old informally developed fishing port still be seen by the hurried visitor.

Repairs and rebuildings by natives and summer visitors; repainting, clapboarding, and new wall-shinglings by the stiff-necked "Headers"; with clumsy-carpentered replacements, entirely lacking the old character that has made this town so attractive to visitors in the past, still goes doggedly on, year after year,—until now there remain only a few of the many picturesque groupings that formerly abounded on every side. Such glimpses as of the North Church tower from Lower Washington St. or the view nearly behind that place, across the back yards off Pearl St. the bit to be seen on the S-shaped zig-zag down the hill from Lee St. onto Front although now much less interesting than before the old fish-warehouse was "slicked up" a few years ago!—or, finally, and most characteristically, the old lobsterman's shack surrounded by lobster pots and dories, down near the "Little Harbor" beach, are fast disappearing, along with other well-remembered vistas—such as the old "Spite House" before it was painted a few years ago. They now linger in the memories of a few older inhabitants, a fewer number of old visitors,—and where they have been recorded for posterity, as vanishing records from the nation's picturesque and "functional" past.

HEAD OF FRONT STREET   ACROSS THE BACK YARDS OFF PEARL STREET

TWO OF THE MANY PICTURESQUE GROUPINGS OF BUILDINGS IN MARBLEHEAD, MASSACHUSETTS

BANQUET ROOM
JEREMIAH LEE MANSION—1768—BANK SQUARE, MARBLEHEAD, MASSACHUSETTS

FIREPLACE AND PANELING, SECOND FLOOR FAMILY LIVING ROOM
JEREMIAH LEE MANSION—1768—BANK SQUARE, MARBLEHEAD, MASSACHUSETTS

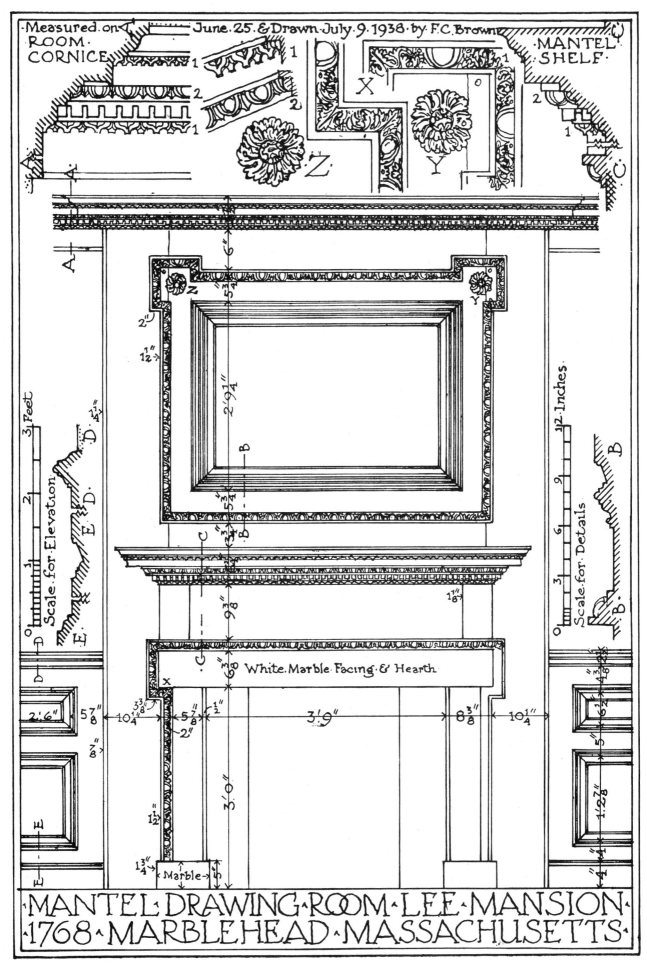

Measured on June 25 & Drawn July 9 1938 by F.C. Brown

ROOM CORNICE

MANTEL SHELF

White Marble Facing & Hearth

Scale for Elevation
3 Feet

Scale for Details
12 Inches

MANTEL·DRAWING·ROOM·LEE·MANSION·
·1768·MARBLEHEAD·MASSACHUSETTS·

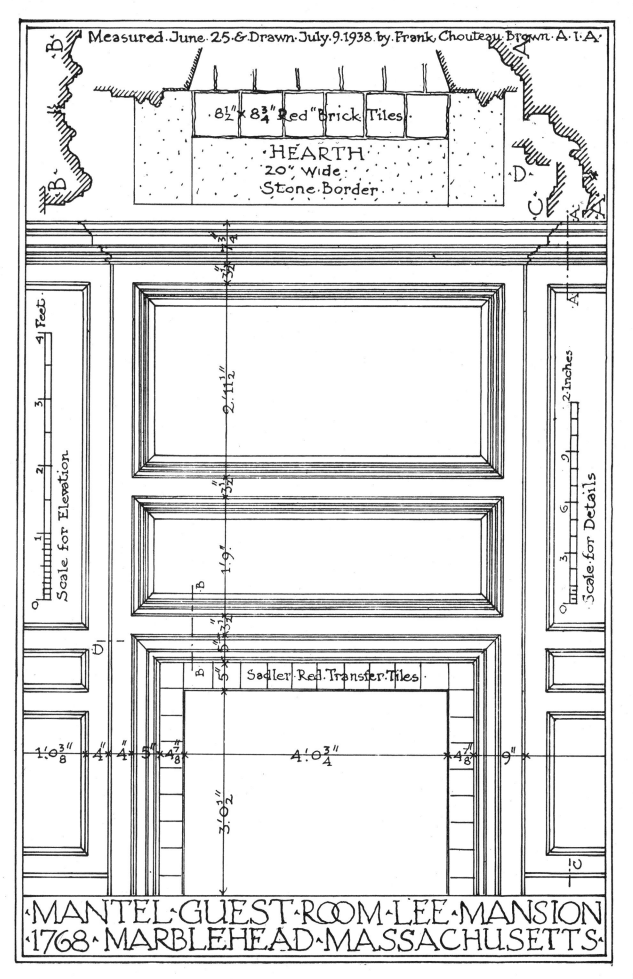

Measured June 25 & Drawn July 9 1938 by Frank Chouteau Brown A.I.A.

$8\frac{1}{2}'' \times 8\frac{3}{4}''$ Red "Brick" Tiles.

HEARTH
20" Wide
Stone Border

4 Feet

Scale for Elevation

$2'.11\frac{1}{2}''$

$3'.3\frac{1}{4}''$
$3'.2''$

$3'.3\frac{1}{2}''$

2 Inches

Scale for Details

1'.9''

Sadler Red Transfer Tiles.

$5''.5''.3\frac{1}{2}''$

$1'.0\frac{3}{8}''$ $4\frac{1}{4}''$ $4\frac{1}{4}''$ 5'' $4\frac{7}{8}''$ $4'.0\frac{3}{4}''$ $4\frac{7}{8}''$ 9''

$3'.0\frac{1}{2}''$

MANTEL·GUEST·ROOM·LEE·MANSION
·1768·MARBLEHEAD·MASSACHUSETTS·

Mantel—Drawing Room   Mantel—Dining Room

JEREMIAH LEE MANSION—1768—BANK SQUARE, MARBLEHEAD, MASSACHUSETTS

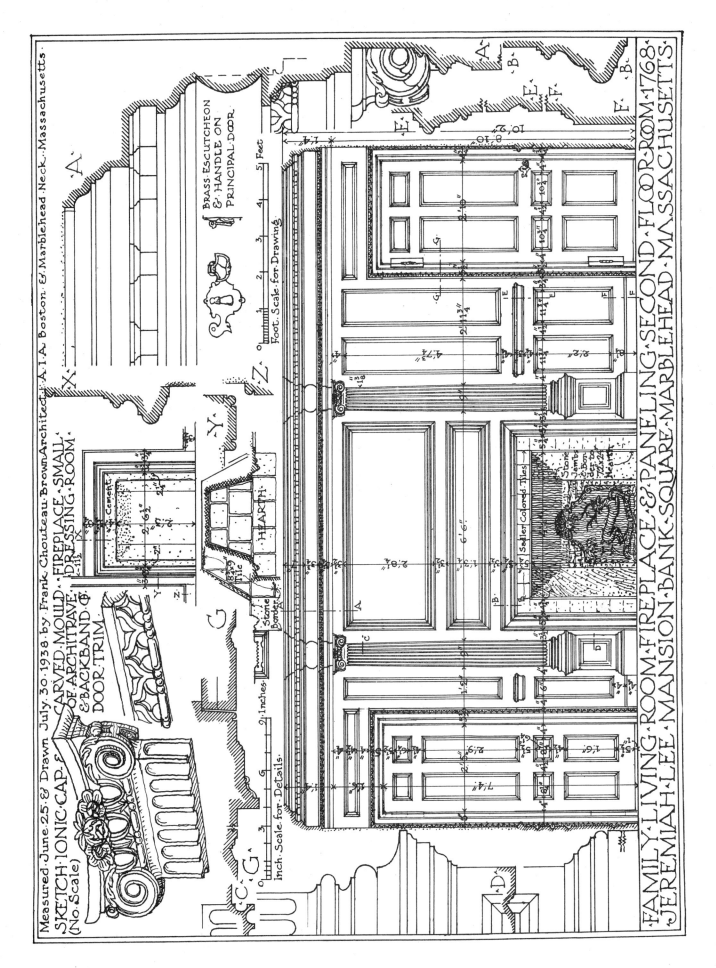

Measured June 25 & Drawn July 30 1938 by Frank Chouteau Brown Architect A I A Boston & Marblehead Neck Massachusetts

SKETCH IONIC CAP &
CARVED MOULD FIREPLACE SMALL
OF ARCHITRAVE DRESSING ROOM
& BACKBAND OF
DOOR TRIM
(No Scale)

BRASS ESCUTCHEON
& HANDLE ON
PRINCIPAL DOOR

FAMILY LIVING ROOM FIREPLACE & PANELING SECOND FLOOR ROOM 1768
JEREMIAH LEE MANSION BANK SQUARE MARBLEHEAD MASSACHUSETTS

THE KITCHEN   CORNER OF BANQUET ROOM

JEREMIAH LEE MANSION—1768—BANK SQUARE, MARBLEHEAD, MASSACHUSETTS

"The Gun House"   Lower Washington Street, Looking North
GLIMPSES OF OLD BUILDINGS WHICH ABOUND IN MARBLEHEAD, MASSACHUSETTS

BUTMAN HOUSE—1760—ROCKPORT, MASSACHUSETTS

FRANCIS ("RED CAP") NORWOOD HOUSE—1700-20—
OVERLOOKING HARBOR, ROCKPORT, MASSACHUSETTS

Cottages of Cape Ann

The early Colonial cottage, wherever it may still be found unspoiled by later additions and changes, possesses a charm and attraction that is not always conveyed by its larger and more formal dwelling associate. Usually of only one story, or a "story and a half" in height, it generally contains only two to three rooms upon the first floor, and its plan is of the simplest—an entrance near one end, a room along what remains of the front, and the rear space divided into two rooms in width.

When the plan is of less depth than that required for two rooms, the entrance may be nearer the middle of the front, and a room at either side; or, if the door and stairs remain near one end, there may be an ell extended at one side, instead of at the rear, as is more likely to be the case with a larger type of plan. And frequently these ells are either built on at later dates, or even a shed moved up against the cottage and connected with it—usually performing the function of a service or kitchen addition.

The upper story may be left unfinished, or divided into a couple of rooms—rarely more, as the dormers now found in the sloping roofs are almost invariably of a date subsequent to the original construction. The chimney—overlarge for its diminutive plan—was generally placed back of the hall and stairway, as was the custom with the larger houses of the period. In

that location it could serve the two larger rooms, of which one was the kitchen—or combined kitchen and living room—and the other a sleeping room off the kitchen, found in so many of the larger dwellings.

The earliest type has already been shown in the original Riggs House of squared logs with a pitch roof. And the same dwelling shows, in its later addition, the gambrel-roof type that came into local fashion just about the end of the Seventeenth Century, and continued to be the almost invariable arrangement until well past the middle of the Eighteenth. Between about 1690 and 1760, almost all the smaller dwellings on "the Cape" were of either the steep or flat gambrel design; by far the larger number being of the comfortable squat outline.

This early squat gambrel roof gradually became steeper and sharper in pitch, until it was succeeded by a flatter single-slope pitched roof near the end of the Eighteenth Century, which, with its smaller chimney, soon came to mark the cottage of the early Nineteenth. Perhaps the dormers covered by a simple extension of the upper roof slope may have been the earlier type—though even they are seldom to be found occurring in the original construction of the Cape cottage. They were probably soon succeeded by the gable-fronted dormer treatment, of which the most authentic and earliest example to be seen in this group

LANGFORD HOMESTEAD—ABOUT 1760—LANESVILLE, MASSACHUSETTS

of illustrations is the dormer on the "Cottage at the Head of the Cove" in Annisquam.

And so, too, the very modesty of these early cottage dwellings makes it difficult to find many whose early history and exact date of construction are known. Usually one is dependent upon some family legend, or the stories carried down to some existing "early inhabitant" by his elders, for a clue to the early ownership or records of these simple dwellings.

Cape Ann—named by Prince Charles after his mother, Anne of Denmark, wife of James I—extends about eight miles into the Atlantic, separating Massachusetts and Ipswich Bays, and has an area of about forty-three square miles. The entire coast line is very irregular, and starting at "The Cut"—a short canal cut at an early date to connect the tip of Squam River with Gloucester Harbor—its margin is occupied by a continuous settlement, the principal sections of which are known by many descriptive local names, such as, Riverdale, Annisquam, Bay View, Lanesville, Folly Cove, Pigeon Cove, Sandy Bay (now Rockport), Straitsmouth, Land's End, Long Beach, Bass

Rocks, East Gloucester, and the Harbor. On the interior are the Farms and the legendary ruins of Dogtown Common, while a considerable area of land upon the mainland is also known as West Gloucester, extending toward Essex and Ipswich and along the Magnolia Shore.

About 1700, or soon thereafter, one Joshua Norwood came and settled on Gully Point, Straitsmouth, near Land's End, where he built a log cabin, which was afterwards removed to Dock Square, where it now stands at one side of Atlantic Avenue; with the Hannah Jumper house upon the other, the two being among the oldest cottages in Rockport. The rough log construction of the former may still be seen inside.

Nearby, the gambrel-roofed cottage of Francis ("Red Cap") Norwood still overlooks the harbor from its old location back from the more modern Atlantic Avenue. It was built about 1720, and its large central chimney contains the two largest fireplaces in the town. From Dock Square, the main road to Land's End is first known as Mt. Pleasant, then as South Street, and this section is usually called Cove

"OLD TARR HOMESTEAD"—6 SOUTH STREET, ROCKPORT, CAPE ANN, MASSACHUSETTS

GAMAGE HOUSE, HIGH STREET—ABOUT 1725—ROCKPORT, CAPE ANN, MASSACHUSETTS

LANE HOMESTEAD—ABOUT 1825—ANNISQUAM, MASSACHUSETTS

Hill, and leads to the "South End." "No. Six South Street," built well before 1750, probably about 1725, is a typical gambrel-roof cottage, which has been unusually well cared for and preserved. While just across Prospect Street is another old cottage, originally belonging either to an early Poole or another Tarr family offshoot, which has been recently restored. Farther along South Street is a veritable *congerie* of Smith, Poole, and Tarr family dwellings, all dating from about 1750 to 1775.

Most of the small dwellings that once crowded the lanes and streets of Gloucester and Rockport have been replaced by the newer buildings and "improvements" called for by the prosperity and growing business of these centers, but a few still remain tucked away in the older streets and back corners of the towns, where business has not yet come to disturb them.

As was so often the case, these little cottages were originally built facing to the south, at a time when there were no established streets—and even the main travelled roads were an informal and movable element in the community, the houses being most usually approached across fields or woodlands by means of a footpath. It has been the fate of many of these original homesteads to be later turned into the kitchen or service portions of larger houses, later built to front the streets—as in the old Woodbury cottage.

Most frequently—where still upon their original foundations—they now stand at all angles to later-day streets, which—particularly upon "the Cape"—wind their way about, while avoiding the sturdy ledge outcroppings and irregular boulder-droppings left by the terminal moraine that scarred and grooved the contours of the township. Latter-day dwellings may front primly upon street and square; and often jostle the corners of their older associates in the doing o't; but the little dwellings of the earlier generations remain undisturbed and placid among them, secure in their possession of that same vague but unescapable "it," that is so woefully lacking in the construction of later generations, particularly the houses—of whatever size— built from about 1830.

In fact, one rather suspects that some part of their compositional charm may come from this very informality of relation to the street lines before them; forcing that glimpse of the front at an angle that shows the spectator also a considerable part of the house-end gable—this being rather an advantage than a disadvantage in the general appearance and appeal made by these unpretentious dwellings.

JOSHUA NORWOOD'S CABIN,
ROCKPORT, MASSACHUSETTS
Known as "The Oldest House in Rockport"

OLD WOODBURY HOUSE—ABOUT 1665-70—
ANNISQUAM, MASSACHUSETTS
Now Kitchen Ell Back of Main House

"OLD COTTAGE AT HEAD OF THE COVE"—APP. 1725—ANNISQUAM, CAPE ANN, MASSACHUSETTS

OLD POOLE (CAPT. TARR) COTTAGE—1750-60—ROCKPORT, MASSACHUSETTS

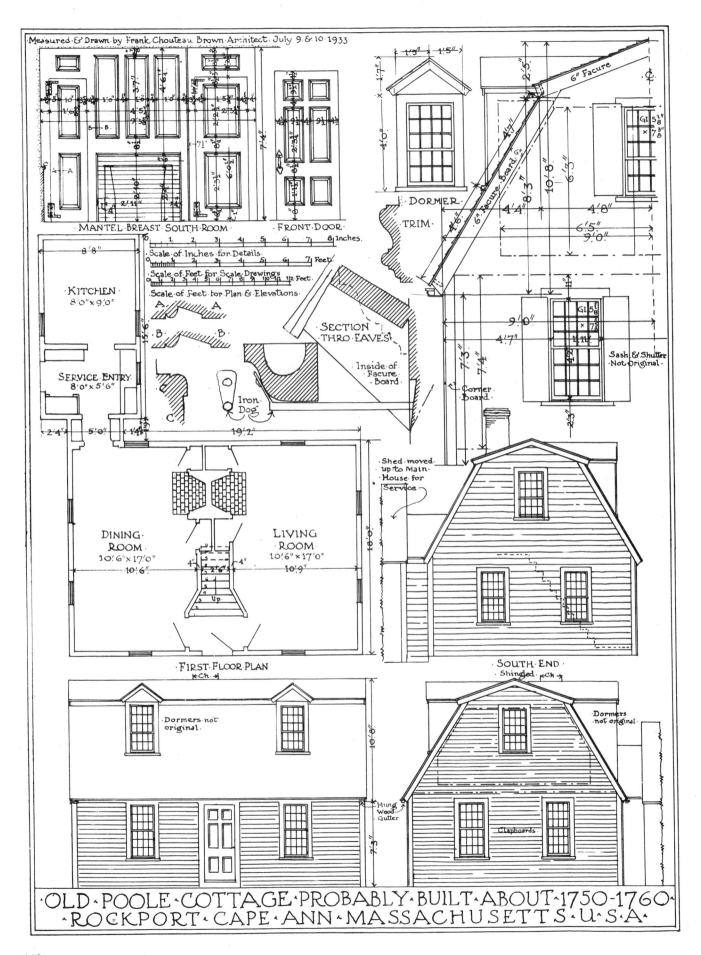

Measured & Drawn by Frank Chouteau Brown Architect July 9 & 10 1933

MANTEL·BREAST·SOUTH·ROOM

FRONT·DOOR

DORMER TRIM

6" Facure

Scale of Inches for Details

Scale of Feet for Scale Drawings

Scale of Feet for Plan & Elevations

SECTION THRO EAVES

Inside of Facure Board

Iron Dog

KITCHEN
8'0" x 9'0"

SERVICE·ENTRY
8'0" x 5'6"

DINING ROOM
10'6" x 17'0"
10'6"

LIVING ROOM
10'6" x 17'0"
10'9"

Up

FIRST·FLOOR·PLAN
←Ch→

Corner Board

Sash & Shutter Not Original.

Shed moved up to Main House for Service

SOUTH·END
Shingled ←Ch→

Dormers not original.

Dormers not original

Hung Wood Gutter

Claphoards

·OLD·POOLE·COTTAGE·PROBABLY·BUILT·ABOUT·1750-1760·
·ROCKPORT·CAPE·ANN·MASSACHUSETTS·U·S·A·

COTTAGE ON WALNUT STREET—
LAST HALF 18TH CENTURY—
ANNISQUAM, MASSACHUSETTS

CLARK COTTAGE, 8 BEACON STREET—ABOUT 1750—GLOUCESTER, MASSACHUSETTS

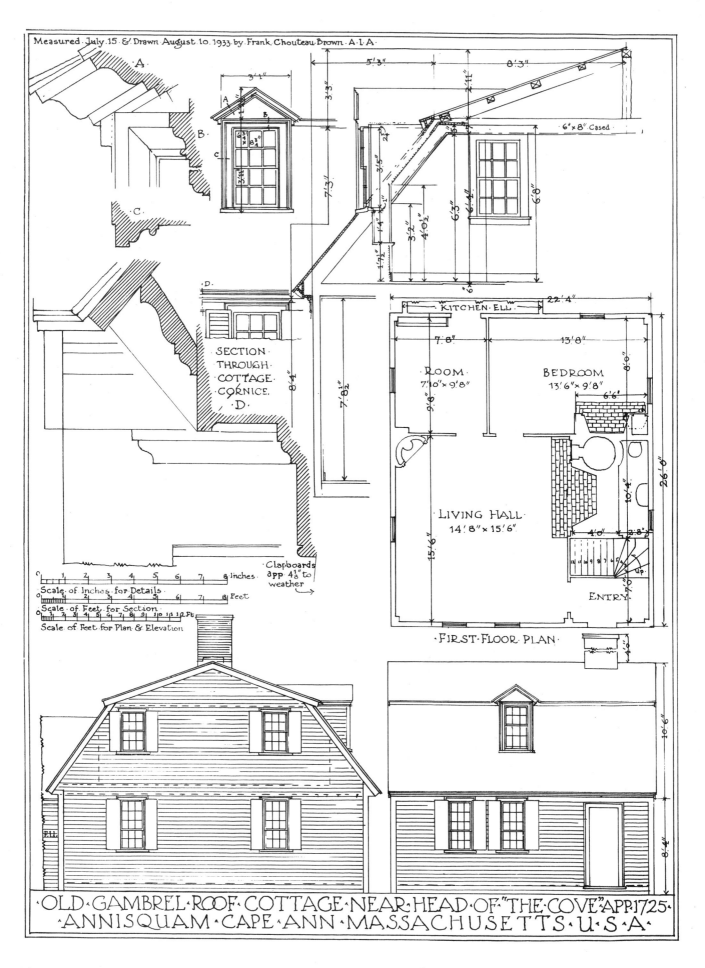

Measured July 15 & Drawn August 10 1933 by Frank Chouteau Brown A.I.A.

SECTION
THROUGH
COTTAGE
CORNICE
D

Clapboards app 4⅛" to weather

Scale of Inches for Details
Scale of Feet for Section
Scale of Feet for Plan & Elevation

KITCHEN ELL

ROOM
7'10" x 9'8"

BEDROOM
13'6" x 9'8"

LIVING HALL
14'8" x 15'6"

ENTRY

FIRST FLOOR PLAN

6" x 8" Cased

OLD GAMBREL ROOF COTTAGE NEAR HEAD OF "THE COVE" APP. 1725
ANNISQUAM CAPE ANN MASSACHUSETTS U.S.A.

COTTAGE BACK OF OLD BURYING GROUND—1750—ROCKPORT, MASSACHUSETTS

OLD COTTAGES BESIDE ROAD TO EAST GLOUCESTER, MASSACHUSETTS

GAMBREL END COTTAGE WITH "JUTBY"—MAIN STREET, PIGEON COVE, MASSACHUSETTS

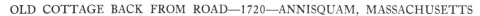

OLD COTTAGE BACK FROM ROAD—1720—ANNISQUAM, MASSACHUSETTS

CAPT. WOODBURY HOUSE, FOLLY COVE, CAPE ANN, MASSACHUSETTS

Fireplace in Dining Room (Old Kitchen)
OLD TARR HOMESTEAD—1750—ROCKPORT, CAPE ANN, MASSACHUSETTS

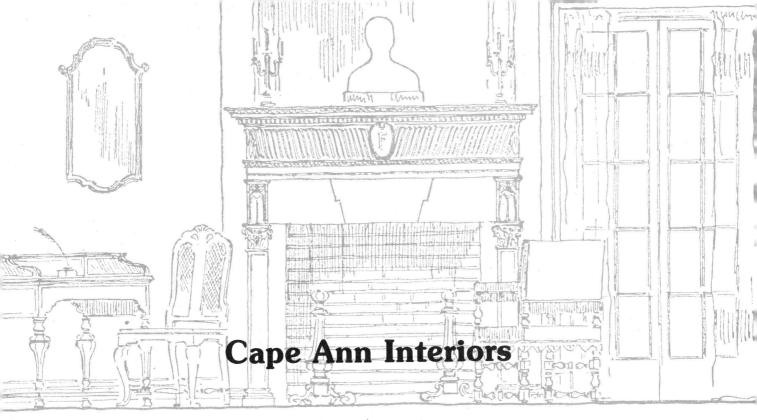

Cape Ann Interiors

After having recognized all those elements that go to make up the picturesqueness and informality of appeal possessed by the simpler types of early dwellings that we usually recall by the use of the term "Cottage"; one must as well realize that these same factors may be extended within doors to help render these same dwellings as reposeful and satisfying to their occupants as they appear to the casual visitor or passerby from without. Many of the elements remain the same. Always is there evident simplicity and informality; the lack of pretense or any attempt at artifice or intentional assumption of superiority. Instead they radiate an atmosphere of homeliness; of everyday comfort and use; of simplicity and friendliness. All this becomes evident from the first glance at the low and inviting entrance; the low-lying roof, set close over the first floor windows; the windows themselves, broken up into many small and beautifully-proportioned panes widened by their open shutters of heavy blinds and narrow intervening wall spaces. The first floor itself is set close down upon the ground. Even if the plan is more spacious than at first seems possible, the depth of the house is not felt because of the flattened gambrel that is so consistent and frequent a part of their design; and has so much to do with making them appear intimate and hospitable.

Deriving, as so many of them do, from an early period—when the conventions of village life were simple and its conveniences slight, they reflect upon their exterior the low ceiling heights and close-grouped windows that in turn do so much to make their small —yet usually ample—interiors seem cosy and home-like; shutting out the outdoors sufficiently, while making its human occupants comfortable beside the warm hearth and wide fireplace that so dominates the principal living room.

The very spacing of the windows themselves— usually set farther away from the house corners upon the exterior than would at first seem pleasing or necessary—upon the interior show that this suggestion of clustering, not only gives better wall space backing for the customary furniture of the family, but also tends to increase the atmosphere of comfort and seclusion.

And that small, almost minuteness of, scale! A scale that takes cognizance of the necessities of the human form—and but little more. Doors of a bare six feet of needed height! (Often one wonders what became of the large and gangling Yankee of tradition —and, for that matter—of established fact and record, as well!) Windows whose tops but barely permit the standing human visage to peer forth without an humbling of the body—if not the spirit!—and leave no room whatever for the continually lowered and hiding shades of but a few generations ago.

Yet the moldings are never small and petty, as is so frequently the case in modern work. Their sections are satisfyingly full bodied, and restfully ample, sturdy and mannish in feel. They are never nervous or disturbing; and especially when they have been allowed to remain without paint, toned only by exposure to the light, and warmed by the patina of time and use, they possess such individuality as warms the owner's life and gives rest to his soul.

Certainly, no one can visit many of these dwellings,

STAIR WELL—COTTAGE AT HEAD OF
"THE COVE," ANNISQUAM, MASSACHUSETTS

In this same house may be found, in the upper story, an end paneled into the gambrel slope of the roof; while the Francis Norwood cottage in Rockport provides two similar second-story paneled ends, of which a few other examples also still exist about the neighborhood—all evidently dating well back into an early and primitive "Cape" period previous to 1750. And in these unpretentious types of cottage building, again, only a notable pride of craftsmanship along with an owner's innate interest—combined with a certain proportion of leisure time—would seem to warrant such unusual expenditures of labor, time, thought and pains upon comparatively unimportant rooms in these unpretentious and modest homes.

Often the marine customs of their builders and inhabitants is evidenced by the informal stair guidance supplied by a piece of rope or cable, reeved through a ring at top and bottom of a steep stair flight, and held in place by some elaborately knotted device worked out upon the separated strands of the rope's ends. This sort of handrail is sometimes locally found, in conjunction with a steeply rising flight of steps such as could only have been inspired originally by some compact and shipshape schooner's cabin scuttle.

Sometimes the staircases pile steeply upward, in one short steep run, from entrance floor to dormered rooms above; sometimes they make the single winding turn of the old Tarr Homestead, against the large

however cursorily, without being forced to accept the persisting legend that they must have been built and occupied in large part by the same owners and builders as worked upon the sailing vessels of the time. They still reflect the compactness and details of the pinks and pinnaces, the sloops and schooners, brigs and barks, that were then being built and outfitted along the shores of these landlocked coves and harbors.

In proof of this conclusion, one has merely to regard the careful workmanship and expert joining to be found in the paneling and dado sections, the doors and mantels, of any of these older cottage dwellings. Who but an owner-carpenter, delighting in the problems of his trade and the use of his hands during long winter days and evenings, would work out so lovingly the charming moldings and ornaments of these interior details, the soft flowing outlines of the cupboard standards, the handworked—almost to say "hand carved" and enriched—moldings along mantelshelf and cupboard cornice? Who else would think out such minor refinements and conveniences as the "transom panel" over the Kitchen-Living Room door in the Annisquam Cottage, for instance—to give added ventilation and circulation in both hot summer days and nights, or in the long cold winters.

And, again, the heavy latticing of the second-story stair well guards—with irregularly cut and fitted cross pieces, set at no uniform or established degree of slope; but yet proportioned with exceptional feeling for the scale of its surroundings and a nice adaptation to place.

ENTRY—COTTAGE AT HEAD OF "THE COVE,"
ANNISQUAM, MASSACHUSETTS

STAIRWAY—FRANCIS NORWOOD HOUSE,
ROCKPORT, MASSACHUSETTS

buttressed chimney of the early century. If so, the
earlier examples may often be as simple as this instance;
where the only change has been the insertion of a
single wide board to fill in the space between the
running rails that were originally open; and are also
often found with added later balusters as has been
done in the Francis Norwood House.

The Tarr Homestead has been far less disturbed
than most of its sister dwellings, and so still provides
the several charming views that go to illustrate some
of the several elements claimed in these accompanying
words, to make these cottages distinctive over their
more formal brethren.

The interiors of both this Tarr Homestead and
the Annisquam Cottage, however, are rarely interesting from the success with which the owners have
found and arranged fittings consistent with the early
period and use of these homes.

In Annisquam, the "Cottage at the Head of the
Cove" (and while there are several "coves" in Annisquam, there is only one "THE Cove"!) gains in
atmosphere by still displaying the tone and charm of
its early pine natural woodwork. From the very
moment one steps inside the simple doorway, to
glimpse the winding stair turn disappearing round the
bend back of the original wide brown boards that
shelter it—till one leaves it again with a last backward
look, this hallway entrance—which is here reduced to

its ultimate minima of attributes—remains nevertheless wholly gratifying merely from its inherent structural integrity, straightforwardness, and obvious fitness
and fineness of proportion throughout.

The adjoining Living Room-Kitchen is equally satisfying—and even more appropriate and perfect in its
fitments and equipment; rugs, furniture, ironwork,
cupboard—taken down from upstairs in this same
house. The old "sinkroom," has been changed into a
more modernly useful "Breakfast Room," with the
gleam of pewter furbishing up its old wall dresser; and
beside it the tiny yet satisfyingly proportioned and de-
tailed small bedroom, off the main Living Room.

And then upstairs, the more dignified and almost
pretentious comfort of a Guest Bedroom, with its
own paneled end, vying in beauty and completeness
with its lower floor counterpart—and with a cornice
mold even to better it, belike! And it is here, where
the interior aspect of the simple dormer is so consistently simple and satisfying, that it is born in upon
the beholder that it can hardly have been so well
carried out if it had not been original to the house.

How sad it is that so few have come down to our
time unaltered and unchanged. Their very simplicity
and apparent humbleness has made them peculiarly the
victims of circumstance, and the unintelligent owner.
They have so often fallen into most unfeeling hands.
No record of their existence and history has usually
been kept. Only occasionally have we exact knowledge of their early owners, or their dates of origin.

STAIRWAY—OLD TARR HOMESTEAD,
ROCKPORT, CAPE ANN, MASSACHUSETTS

COTTAGE AT HEAD OF "THE COVE"—1700-25—ANNISQUAM, CAPE ANN, MASSACHUSETTS

COTTAGE AT HEAD OF "THE COVE"—1700-25—ANNISQUAM, MASSACHUSETTS

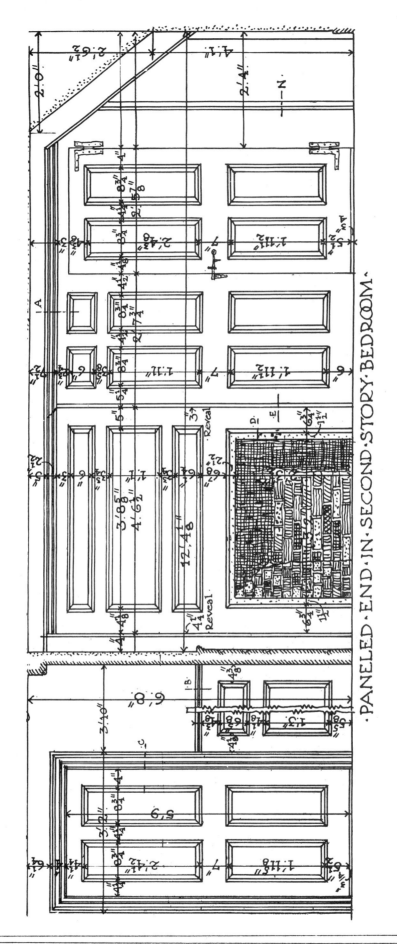

PANELED·END·IN·SECOND·STORY·BEDROOM·

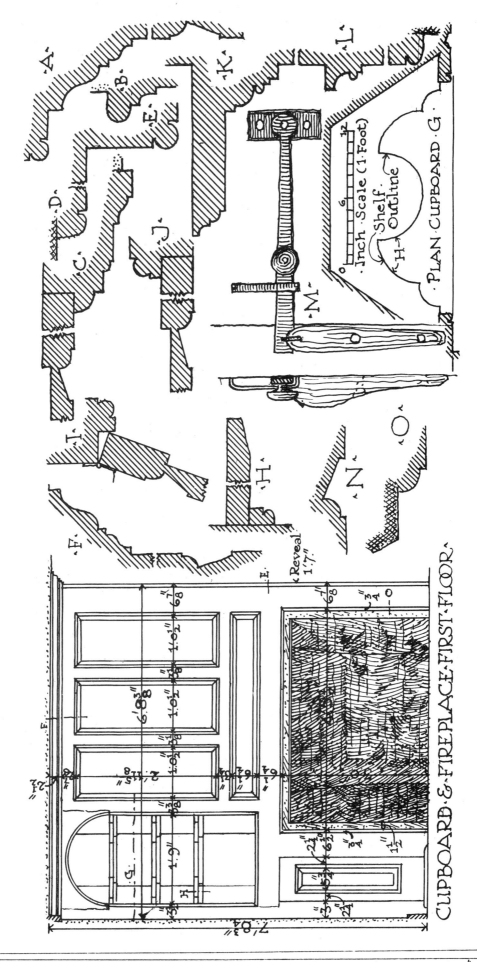

·A·
·B·
·K·
·L·
·E·
·D·
·C·
·J·
·F·
·I·
·H·
·N·
·O·
·M·

·Reveal· 1'7"·

Inch·Scale (1 Foot)
0   6   12
Shelf·
Outline
·H·
·PLAN·CUPBOARD·G·

·G·
·H·
·E·

2'11⅝"
6'8⅜"
1'0⅛"
6'8¾"
1'0¾"
6'8½"
1'0⅞"
2½"
6¾" 6¾"
1'9"
6⅛" 6⅛"
2¼" 2¼"
5¼"
3½"
3¼"
11½"
1'0¾"
6'8¾"
6½"
7'0¾"

·CUPBOARD·&·FIREPLACE·FIRST·FLOOR·

·THREE·MANTELS·OR·PANELED·ENDS·COTTAGE·HEAD·OF·THE·COVE·
·1720·25·ANNISQUAM·CAPE·ANN·MASSACHUSETTS·U·S·A·

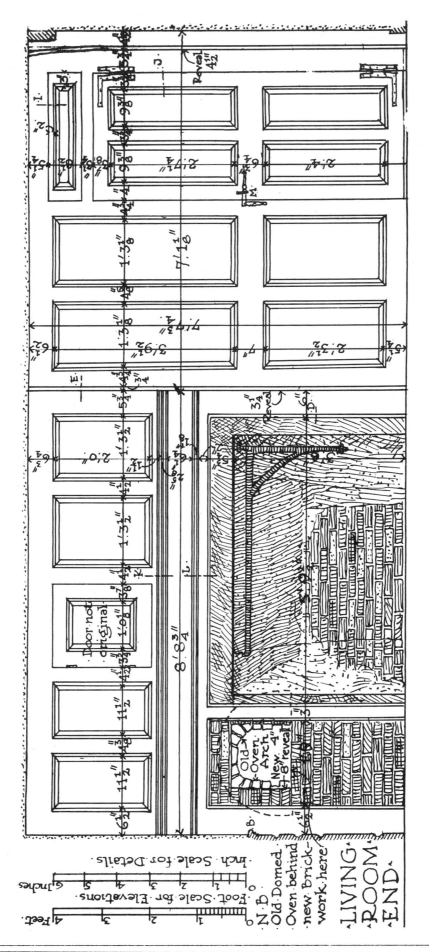

Inch Scale for Details.

5 inches 4 3 2 1 0

Foot Scale for Elevations.

4 feet 3 2 1 0

N.B.
Old Domed
Oven behind
new brick-
work here.

·LIVING·
·ROOM·
·END·

Door not original.

Old
Oven
Arch.
New 4"
8" reveal

Reveal

Reveal 4½"

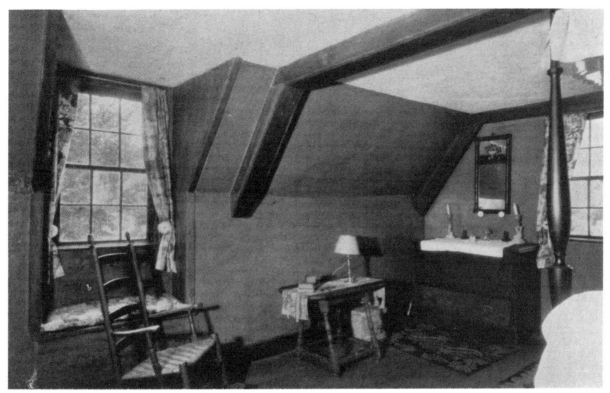

Second Story Bedroom

COTTAGE AT HEAD OF "THE COVE"—1700-25—ANNISQUAM, MASSACHUSETTS

Cupboard and Fireplace—First Floor
COTTAGE AT HEAD OF "THE COVE"—1700-25—ANNISQUAM, MASSACHUSETTS

Fireplace and Mantel in Living Hall

OLD TARR HOMESTEAD—1750—ROCKPORT, CAPE ANN, MASSACHUSETTS

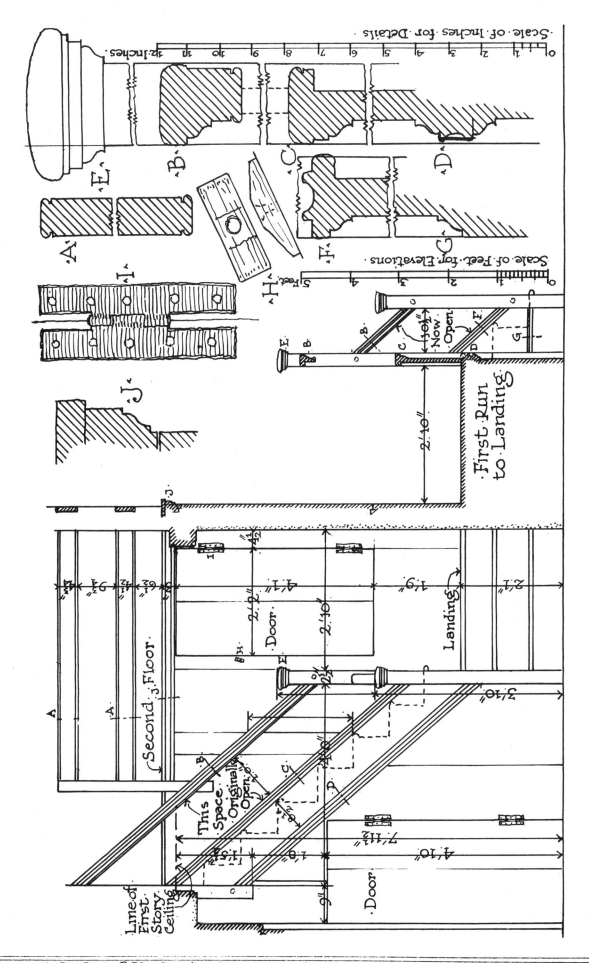

Scale of Inches for Details.

Scale of Feet for Elevations.

First Run to Landing.

Second Floor.

Landing.

Door.

Door.

Line of First Story Ceiling.

This Space Originally Open.

·DETAILS·OF·STAIRCASE·OLD·TARR·HOMESTEAD·CIRCA·1750·
·SOUTH·STREET·ROCKPORT·CAPE·ANN·MASSACHUSETTS·

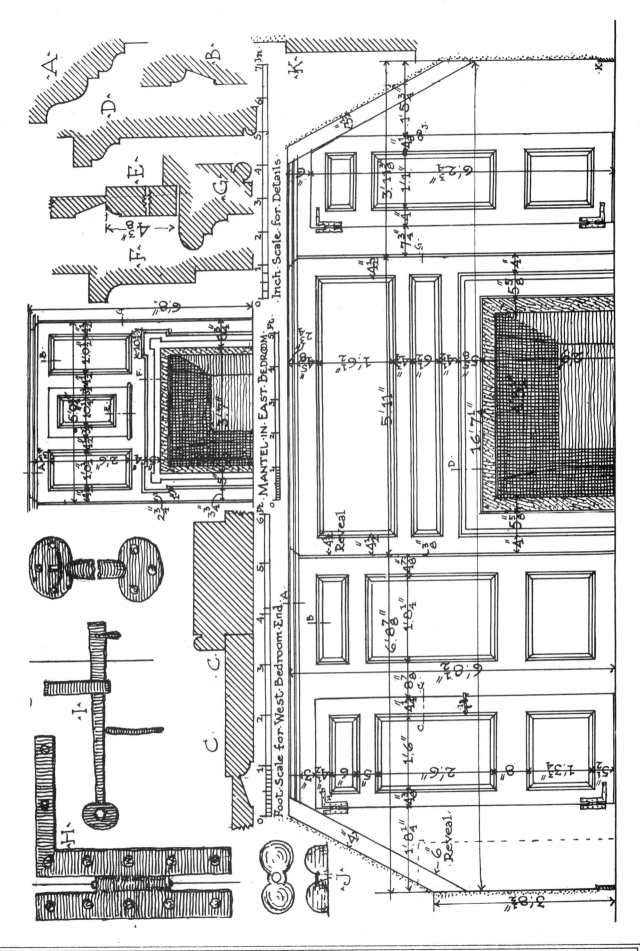

Inch Scale for Details

6 In. MANTEL IN EAST BEDROOM

Foot Scale for West Bedroom End A

·PANELED·INNER·SIDE·OF·WEST·BEDROOM·IN·GAMBREL·1720·
·FRANCIS·NORWOOD·HOUSE·ROCKPORT·MASSACHUSETTS·

Mantel Breast—South Room
OLD POOLE COTTAGE

LIVING ROOM—"OLD TARR HOMESTEAD"—6 SOUTH STREET, ROCKPORT, CAPE ANN, MASSACHUSETTS

FRANCIS ("RED CAP") NORWOOD HOUSE—1700-20—ROCKPORT, CAPE ANN, MASSACHUSETTS

GEORGE GOTT HOUSE—1805—NINE GOTT STREET, ROCKPORT, MASSACHUSETTS

Cape Ann Houses

Some of the simplest yet more dignified examples of these later dwellings are to be found on that portion of the Cape now known as Rockport, which name was given it in 1840, when it was finally set off as a separate town from the then flourishing granite quarries at Pigeon Cove. Previous to that time the district had been known as "Sandy Bay," or was merely called "the Cape" and had been part of Gloucester town since its earliest settlement.

It lies on the eastern part of the Cape, covering an area of about six and one-quarter miles, and is divided into three sections. The North Village, also known as Pigeon Cove, contains the principal quarries; and includes the largest part of the transient population of the region. At the other extremity, towards Straitsmouth and "Lands End," is the section known as the "South End."

There remains only the "Center" where, among the many jetties and wharves, covered with fishermen's "shacks" and artists' studios; the winding streets leading up the rocky slopes to the higher inland country of the Cape, with their old and new houses and cottages, are to be found those few dignified and simple "later houses" remaining on this part of Cape Ann. As a rule these houses were the product of the early fishing industry (at one time two-thirds of the fishing vessels of Cape Ann belonged in Rockport) but one

of the most conspicuous of the town's late houses is the mansion built in 1809 by the Reverend David Jewett, second minister of the First Parish Church.

Probably next in importance among the houses in that locality is the Caleb Norwood, Jr., House (one of at least six "Norwood Houses" in Rockport), standing at the beginning of the slope, at 37 Cove Hill. It belongs to the three-story type of house that was produced in a number of the more prosperous Massachusetts coast communities, few of which are older than the last quarter of the Eighteenth Century.

Nearly opposite, upon a modest street running away from the Harbor, are the two "twin" Gott Houses. They are nearly alike in exterior arrangement and exhibit only minor variations of detail, as will appear from a comparison of the two doorways, although the plans and interior details vary. As a matter of fact, No. 5, the second one to be built, now appears to be the older, possibly largely from the fact that it still possesses the inside "sliding shutters."

A little further up the hill leading toward the "South End" (and so impatient to arrive there that it changes its name no less than four times within a short half-mile of length!) is another remaining Gott Mansion, built in 1770 by one John Gott. This, too, is one of the six or seven three-story dwellings in Rockport, although the upper story was actually added at a later time. The house is of unusual plan, with several staircases and two fireplaces.

Another of the so-called "Norwood Houses" is the Ebenezer Pool House, fronting upon the famous Dock Square, almost at the beginning of "Bear Skin Neck" (now usually spelled the other way!) where artists, bathers, and models cluster so thickly on hot summer days.

It is upon this same square that the old Tavern, with its basement Taproom and second-story ballroom (added in 1838), still stands; although now, alas, the ballroom has been divided into many rooms, and the old archway through which the coaches drove into the

irregular borders of the harbor of Gloucester itself. Here, at one time, were all the houses of the wealthy sea captains or owners of the sailing vessels that then were tied up between voyages at piers located at the water end of the gardens, down which their owners looked from their front doorways on the land side above. At that time the present "Main Street" of Gloucester did not exist. At a much later date it was cut ruthlessly through the old gardens and "front yards" of the big houses perched upon the higher ground above. For a time they were still entered through the old front doorways facing toward the harbor; with a shortened yard, and new fences with

REV. DAVID JEWETT HOUSE—1806-09—MAIN STREET, ROCKPORT, MASSACHUSETTS

inner courtyard has been filled in with a modern shop. It has still more recently become the headquarters of the artists of the vicinity; and who better than they can appreciate the advantages of restoring the former picturesqueness and appeal of this one-time center of community life on this portion of Cape Ann!

Just as the earliest examples of dwellings within the Cape area are still to be found on that portion where the first permanent settlements appear to have been made—the region of Annisquam and West Gloucester —so are the greater number of examples of the more prosperous later periods to be found still about the

gateways and paths leading up from the new street below. Upon the other side of this street lay the warehouses and piers; and gradually business began to encroach upon the land side of the street, with stores built upon the lower ends of the gardens; until today the newer "Main Street" is banked almost solidly along both sides with stores and business blocks, leaving a few of the old houses to be approached through store passageways or small entrance alleys; or forcing those located still higher upon the bank to turn about for entrance access to the next higher street paralleling the harbor, through a new or old doorway

THE CALEB NORWOOD, JR., HOUSE—1775-80—ROCKPORT, MASSACHUSETTS

upon the former rear, or side, of the old dwelling.

The Sargent-Murray-Gilman-Hough House is an example of this progress, except that it has here gone even a step farther; and, of still *more* recent years, the families preserving the house have been able to purchase again the land fronting upon Main Street, and have torn down the new stores and built a new fence, so that it is once again possible to view the front of the house upon its Harbor side. For many years this noble house stood unregarded in the town. It was a tenement for some time, and only a few knew the beauties of the finish its humble rear exterior con-

charm of detail can be seen and appreciated by visitors.

Of course, it has followed that the years of prosperity of the fishing and other related industries in Gloucester has been the cause of the destruction of most all the old houses that once bordered its inner harbor. One still remains, and is used as an Old Ladies' Home; a few others, further away from the more bustling business section of the Main Street, still exist precariously, but only on sufferance, as tenements; often rebuilt, so that many would not even suspect their former magnificence.

Almost beside the "Sawyer Free Library" stands

THE EBENEZER POOL HOUSE—1798—DOCK SQUARE, ROCKPORT, MASSACHUSETTS

cealed. Then it was discovered that John Murray, a minister of the beautiful church built in 1806, and still standing, had once lived in this house. He had married Judith Sargent, daughter of Winthrop Sargent, who was also an ancestor of the late artist, the lamented John Singer Sargent. Aided by those interested in the lives of these two rather strangely combined leaders, the house has been reclaimed, and with surprisingly little change or necessary repair has been placed in a condition where its innate beauty and

the old Mackenzie House at 90 Middle Street, built about 1759, with an unusual treatment about the entrance door. As Middle Street continues its course around the harbor toward the main waterfront, it leads by other houses with exterior and interior beauty, as well as architectural details to commend them to the trained and appreciative eye. One of these is the Capt. John Somes house, with its very characteristic doorway design, shown both in the photograph and the measured drawing. These entrances were chosen for

DOORWAY—5 GOTT STREET (GOTT HOUSE) 1806—ROCKPORT, MASSACHUSETTS

Doorway—83 Main Street
HOUSE AT ROCKPORT, MASSACHUSETTS

Doorway—7 Gott Street
GEORGE GOTT HOUSE—1805—ROCKPORT, MASS.

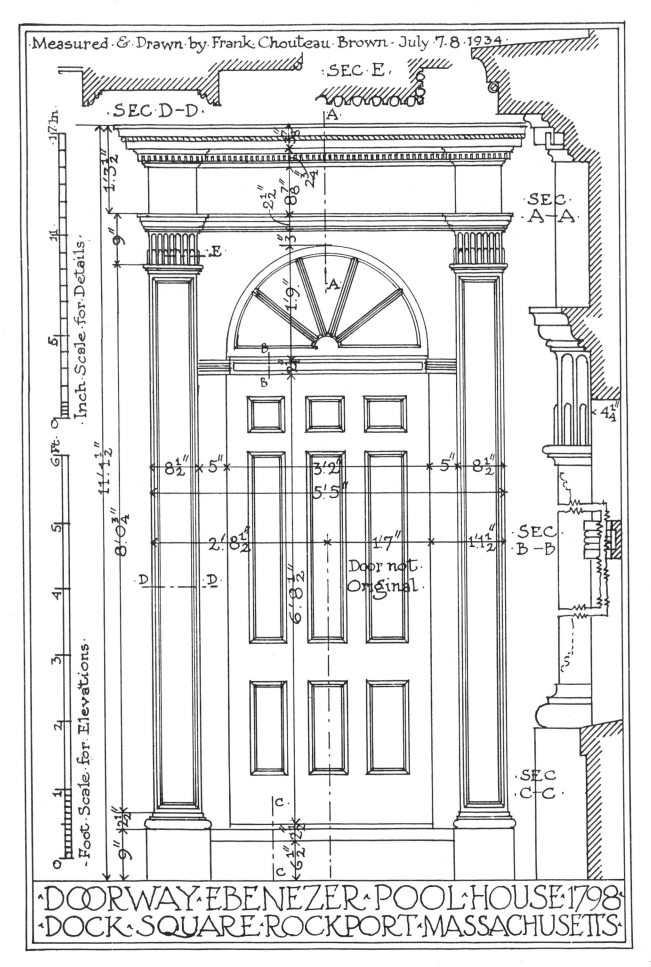

Measured & Drawn by Frank Chouteau Brown · July 7. 8. 1934.

SEC E.

SEC D-D.

SEC A-A

SEC B-B

SEC C-C

·17.in.

·Inch·Scale·for·Details·

·Foot·Scale·for·Elevations·

Door not Original

·DOORWAY·EBENEZER·POOL·HOUSE·1798·
·DOCK·SQUARE·ROCKPORT·MASSACHUSETTS·

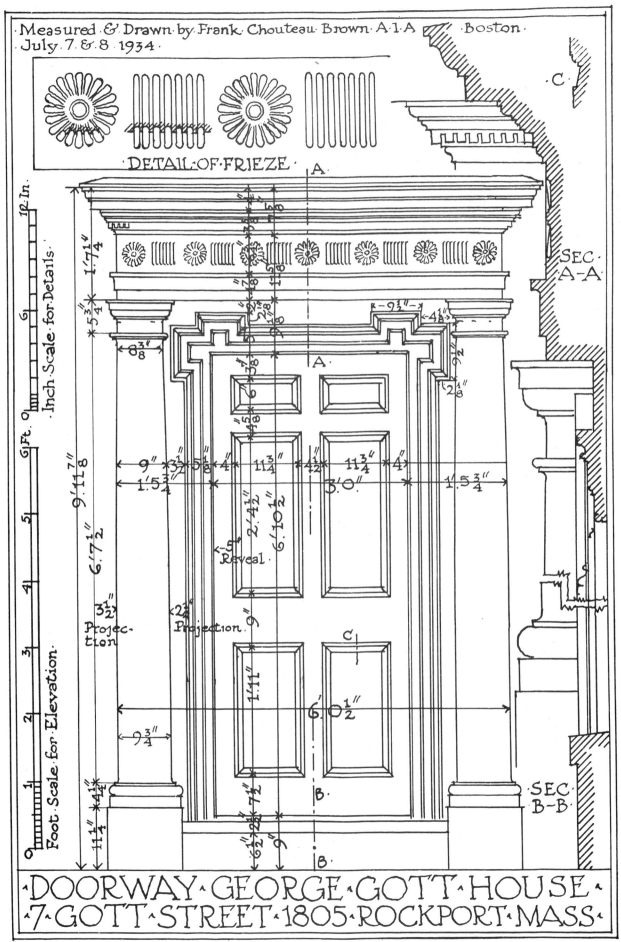

Measured & Drawn by Frank Chouteau Brown A·I·A ·Boston·
·July·7·&·8·1934·

·DETAIL·OF·FRIEZE·

·C·

SEC·
·A-A·

SEC·
·B-B·

·DOORWAY·GEORGE·GOTT·HOUSE·
·7·GOTT·STREET·1805·ROCKPORT·MASS·

12·In.

·Inch·Scale·for·Details·

G·Ft.

·Foot·Scale·for·Elevation·

measuring—in connection with these designs—because they display some of the most individual and local treatments—that recur again and again. This doorway shows jogged treatment of the architrave surrounding the door. Also, it illustrates the boldness of reveal and freedom of handling of well known and understood classical models. A close study of these drawings will show how often the use of a hackneyed or conventional detail of the strict order-formula has been adroitly and successfully avoided. In this very entrance the top of the grooves in the triglyph are ended unusually; the door architrave, cornice, and molded edge (A) of the bracket are not the conventional sections. In the Rockport doorways the details of the pilaster capitals, panels, and molded entablature are at once unusually simple,

delicate, and precise—while the jogged and broken outlines around the door frame of the Gott doorway re-echo that local peculiarity, at the same time that the carved ornamental treatment along the frieze is an unusually well worked out variant of a local model.

Thirty years ago both Rockport and Gloucester contained double or triple the number of examples of interesting Colonial dwelling architecture that they contain today. From Gloucester, particularly, have they vanished—though sometimes they may still be suspected of lurking behind modernly reshingled exterior walls, and the outlines of one of the very oldest houses in the district may still be tantalizingly traced under the exterior camouflage of a plastered and half-timbered face-wall treatment that may be found at the now well-named corner of "Pest House Lane"!

GOTT HOUSE—1770—2 PLEASANT STREET, ROCKPORT, MASSACHUSETTS

THE SARGENT-MURRAY-GILMAN-HOUGH HOUSE—1768—GLOUCESTER, MASSACHUSETTS

HOUSE AT 15 HIGH STREET—1800-20—ROCKPORT, MASSACHUSETTS

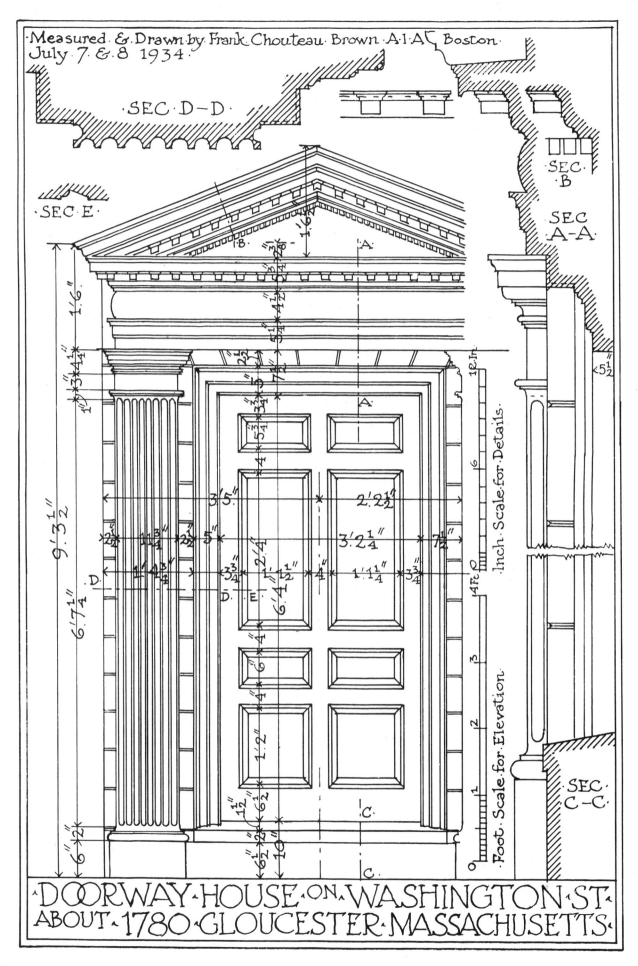

**DOORWAY·HOUSE·ON·WASHINGTON·ST·
ABOUT·1780·GLOUCESTER·MASSACHUSETTS·**

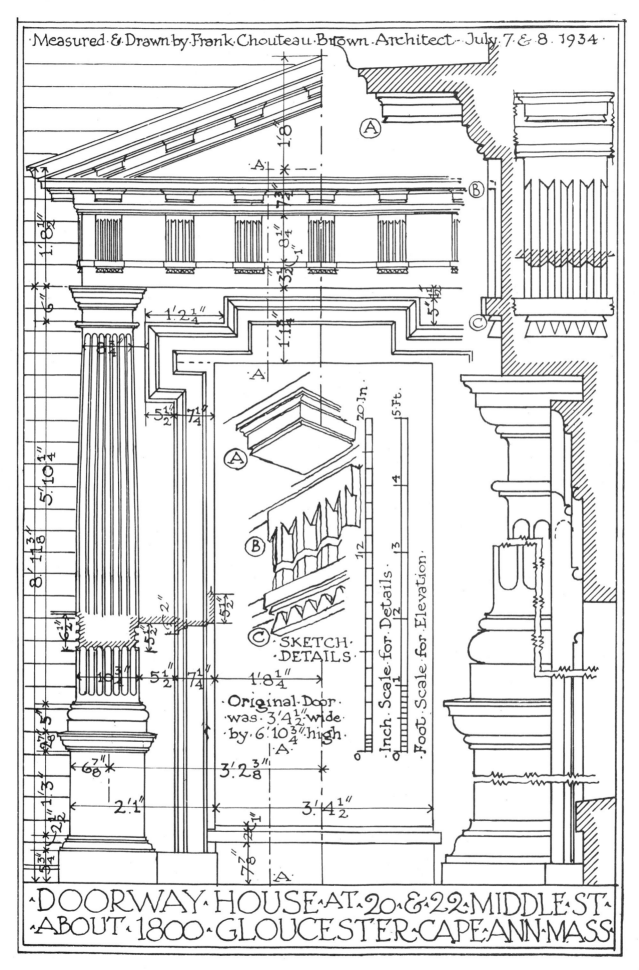

Measured & Drawn by Frank Chouteau Brown Architect. July 7 & 8 1934

A

A

B

C

1'·8"
7½"
8¼"
1'·1"
32"
1'·8½"
6"
8¼"
5'·10¼"
8'·11⅜"
6½"
5½"
5½"
2"
5½"
5½"
7¼"
6⅞"
2'·1"
1'·3"
2½"
5¾"
7⅝"
2'·1"

1'·2¼"
5½"
7¼"
1'·1¼"
5"·4¾"

A
B
C ·SKETCH·
·DETAILS·

20·In.
5·Ft.
12
3
4
1
2
·Inch·Scale·for·Details·
·Foot·Scale·for·Elevation·

·Original·Door·
·was·3'·4½"·wide·
·by·6'·10¾"·high·
A

3'·2⅜"
3'·4½"

·DOORWAY·HOUSE·AT·20·&·22·MIDDLE·ST·
·ABOUT·1800·GLOUCESTER·CAPE·ANN·MASS·

147

Doorway—301 and 303 Washington Street
HOUSE—1780—GLOUCESTER, MASSACHUSETTS

THE BABSON HOUSE—1740—GLOUCESTER, MASSACHUSETTS

Doorway—20 and 22 Middle Street
THE CAPT. JOHN SOMES HOUSE—
1800—GLOUCESTER, MASS.

"OLD COLLINS HOUSE"—1740—254 MAIN STREET, GLOUCESTER, MASSACHUSETTS

THE CAPE ANN SCIENTIFIC, LITERARY, AND HISTORICAL
ASSOCIATION BUILDING—1808—GLOUCESTER, MASSACHUSETTS

FIRST FLOOR PARLOR—THE SARGENT-MURRAY-GILMAN-HOUGH HOUSE—1768—GLOUCESTER, MASSACHUSETTS

The better houses still to be found upon the tip of the Cape—or in the region about Rockport harbor —fall into two general divisions. There is one group about which the legend of "Pirate Gold" persists as the explanation of the source from which the wealth to build them derived—but, alluring as these syllables always are in their appeal, there seems little reason for believing such easily acquired wealth to have been used in their construction—or, if such was actually the case, the dwellings themselves remain as evidence that the source to which their being is still ascribed was hardly as prolific and profitable a one as is usually believed; for they remain as examples of a very simple, direct type of architectural design; quite such as might have been made from the slower and more hardily earned wealth secured from the early fishing fleet that formerly sailed from Rockport and Pigeon Cove; which the buildings themselves would seem to prove to be products of the busy and skillful handiwork of the boatbuilders of that section, as well.

As a matter of actual fact, the better houses of the later period—from about 1760 to 1825—today to be seen in Rockport; are far more expressive of the simplicity and reserve of the New Englanders that created and paid for them, than of any exuberant and flamboyant Pirate spirits! Their interior finish is also of the simplest. Mantels with delicately molded and sometimes chisel-cut ornament upon a few surfaces. Staircases with simple square posts of small size, the balusters usually only of the plain seven-eighths or inch-

and-an-eighth square type, with a simple but delicate end bracket, are rather the rule. Thin six panel doors, with small molded panel edges, and a simple mitred architrave. Occasionally a reeded dado-cap above a single wide pine board appears briefly—but the full paneled ends, with sturdy molded-edge panels, have gone with the earlier period work; and have not persisted into the later period upon this side of the Cape.

Then there are a few unusual examples of a still later style; expressive of the wealth that was briefly derived from the granite quarries that were for some years worked extensively along this coast. This period has expressed itself best perhaps in the several dwellings built of split granite—usually laid up in courses. There remain some barns and out-buildings, a few houses, and one "double cottage"; all built in granite, between about 1825 to 1850. And the interior finish of these houses also continues in carrying on the later simple traditions, established in the immediately preceding period. And within this same time-period lie the few "Neo-Grec" houses scattered about the region; of which four almost exactly alike in design still remain—two in the Rockport-Pigeon Cove region and two in Gloucester.

Turn to the later settlements, built along the Gloucester Harborside, and a quite different story is to be found. Here the lumber industry that had first brought wealth to the settlers upon the rough shores of the Cape, had been supplanted by the fishermen who took up and followed that industry when the earlier fleets of smaller vessels that had previously sailed from Annisquam and Rockport harbors were supplanted by these larger vessels with their homeport in the well protected and deeper waters of the Gloucester bay.

The old buildings of Gloucester have suffered, particularly, by its prosperity and continued business importance. It remains the "shire" town of the region; and so it has been inevitable that as its business has continued to prosper, its older houses have been more and more altered, or adapted to other uses. Many have been turned into stores; others in not quite so busy a neighborhood have merely fallen into disuse or been made into tenements; while still others, in what have remained better neighborhoods, are now owned by wealthy families—or "summer people," and as such, have often been "improved" or "modernized" beyond repair or even sometimes recognition!

Of all these dwellings, the house that was for years the most pretentious and beautiful, was probably that now used as the Sawyer Free Library. Unfortunately, even before it came into the possession of the Library, it had already been much changed and "modernized." The old fence of high wooden pickets that at one time surrounded it, has been taken down and replaced with a costly (and most inartistic) arrangement of cut granite blocks in large sizes; the old paneled and recessed windows have had their sizes enlarged, the sills cut down, and some of the finish changed or removed. The two rooms at the left of the entrance have been entirely torn out, with the old chimney between them, and the finish lost. But of the other front room enough remains to make it an imposing and interesting interior still; though the mantel has been changed. The old staircase is also in place, with the former elaborate landing window.

Across the side street the Mackenzie House still possesses two beautiful paneled ends, on the two right-hand rooms, one above the other; both very similar in design. Another house "across the street" (this time across Middle Street) from the Library, is the Murray-Sargent-Gilman-Hough dwelling. It has been preserved as the home of the founder of Universalism —the first church used by John Murray's congregation having been a small building upon another part of this lot, later replaced by the beautiful church built in 1806 that is still standing nearby. This house also has—in two second floor rooms—paneling nearly alike in design along the fireplace sides of the rooms; which are against the outer walls; the end windows occurring only in what are closets, back of the doors shown in the panelwork! The parlor mantel is quite different from anything else upon the Cape; while the staircase,

although painted, is one of the best examples of the elaborate twisted type in New England; although not done in mahogany—as in the Lee Mansion at Marblehead. The hallway and front rooms of this house were built, along with the kitchen ell and the odd corner fireplace upon the second floor over it, in 1768.

Both these houses are of rather an early date; as is even more true of the well known Babson House, which contains one of the most beautiful all-paneled rooms in the State (and one of the two still remaining upon Cape Ann!) with a most interesting staircase. This house also exhibits three old vestibule entrances.

The "Old Collins House"—now descended to use as a tenement and a storehouse of odds and ends of fishing tackle—had once seen better days as the home of a ship owner facing down upon the heel of the Harbor. It still stands in its old location, now closely hemmed in with stores upon right and left, huddled up against the rocky hillside, as always. A sturdy old staircase and the dominating vigor and boldness of its best rooms are worthy of better things.

Just as Rockport boasts of its "twin" Gott Houses; so has Gloucester also a pair of "twins"; and also built—according to the legend—by two brothers. These two buildings on Pleasant St. were, however, being carried along at the same time—and a certain amount of rivalry was in evidence between both the workmen and the owners; each striving to in some way better the design or workmanship over its competitor (a somewhat different spirit than nowadays dominates the thoughts and ideals of the members of our building "Unions"!) and the story goes that, one morning, the owner of one house, having already nailed up his cornerboards, and rushed the wall clapboarding along ahead of his competitor, arrived upon the scene to find that Col. Jacob Smith "housewright" —his apparently slower neighbor—had been spending the time more elaborately grooving his corner boards into a sort of elaborate "quoining"—rather unusually small in scale—and was even then setting them up into place! "And," as the story goes, dramatically, "he gave one look at them and turned away and never spoke another word to him, from that day to this!" And it is this—the more elaborate of the two houses —that is now the home of the "Cape Ann Scientific, Literary and Historical Association" (all of which is merely long for "Historical Society"). This house dates from 1808; and is an excellent and representative example of that period, as it took shape in the neighborhood and within the area of that rugged and picturesque island that is known as "Cape Ann."

THE SARGENT-MURRAY-GILMAN-HOUGH HOUSE—1768—GLOUCESTER, MASSACHUSETTS

Paneled End in Dining Room Chamber—Second Floor

THE SARGENT-MURRAY-GILMAN-HOUGH HOUSE—1768—GLOUCESTER, MASSACHUSETTS

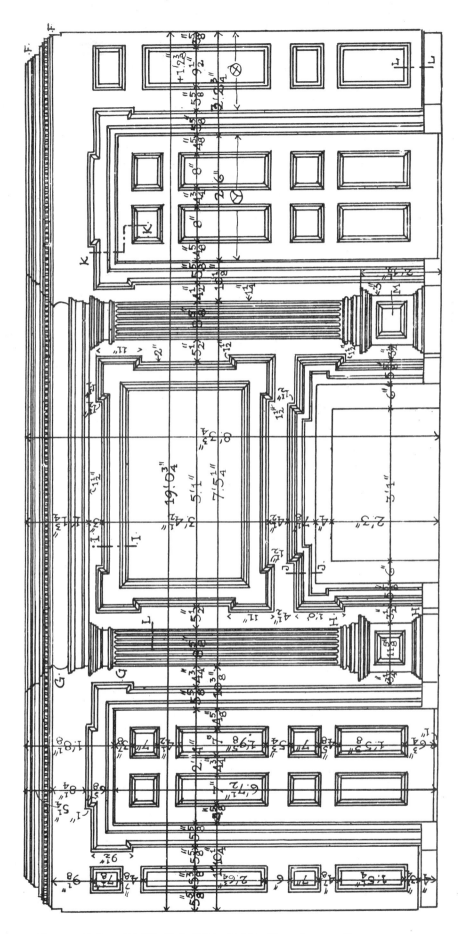

· PANELED · END · IN · DINING · ROOM · CHAMBER ·

· FIREPLACE · IN · SARGENT ~ MURRAY ~ GILMAN ~ HOUGH ·
· HOUSE · 1768 · GLOUCESTER · CAPE · ANN · MASSACHUSETTS ·

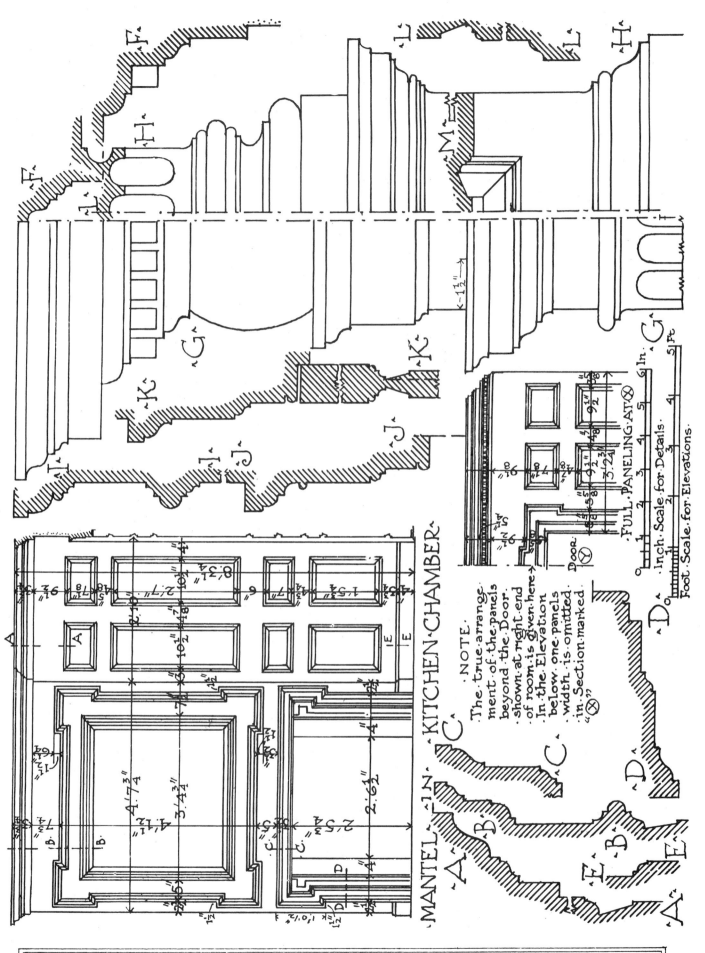

·MANTEL·IN·KITCHEN·CHAMBER·

·NOTE·
The true arrangement of the panels beyond the Door shown at right end of room is given here. In the Elevation below one panels width is omitted in Section marked "⊗"

·FULL·PANELING·AT ⊗

Inch Scale for Details.

Foot Scale for Elevations.

Mantel in Kitchen Chamber

THE SARGENT-MURRAY-GILMAN-HOUGH HOUSE—1768—GLOUCESTER, MASSACHUSETTS

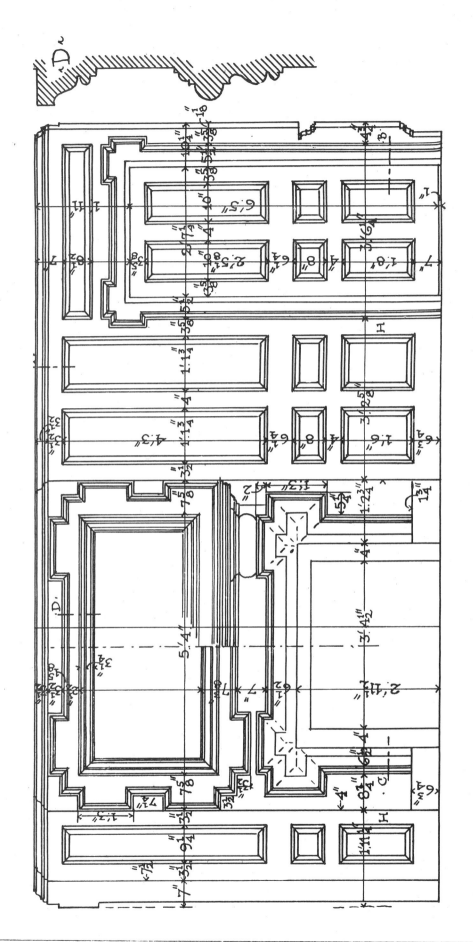

PANELED·ROOM·IN·OLD·COLLINS·HOUSE·"1760~1770·
·GLOUCESTER··CAPE·ANN··MASSACHUSETTS·

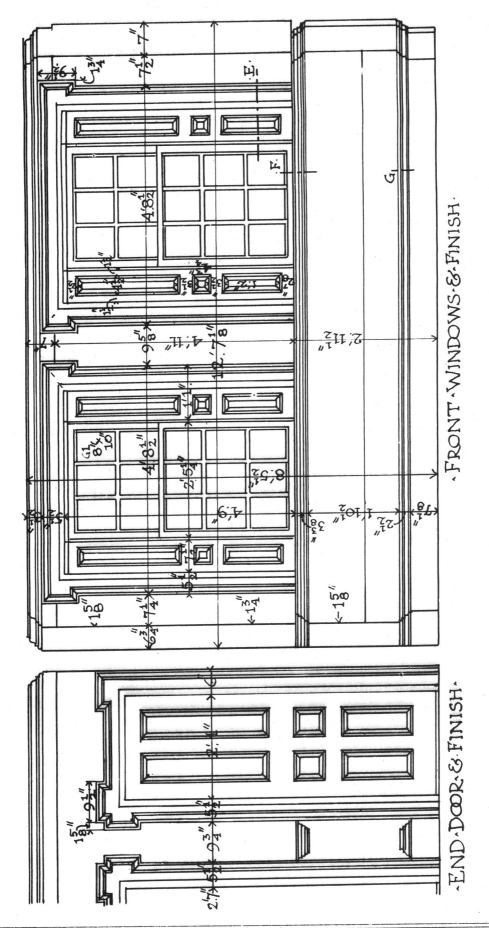

·FRONT·WINDOWS·&·FINISH·

·END·DOOR·&·FINISH·

·PANELED·ROOM·IN·"OLD·COLLINS·HOUSE"·1760-1770·
·GLOUCESTER·CAPE·ANN··MASSACHUSETTS·

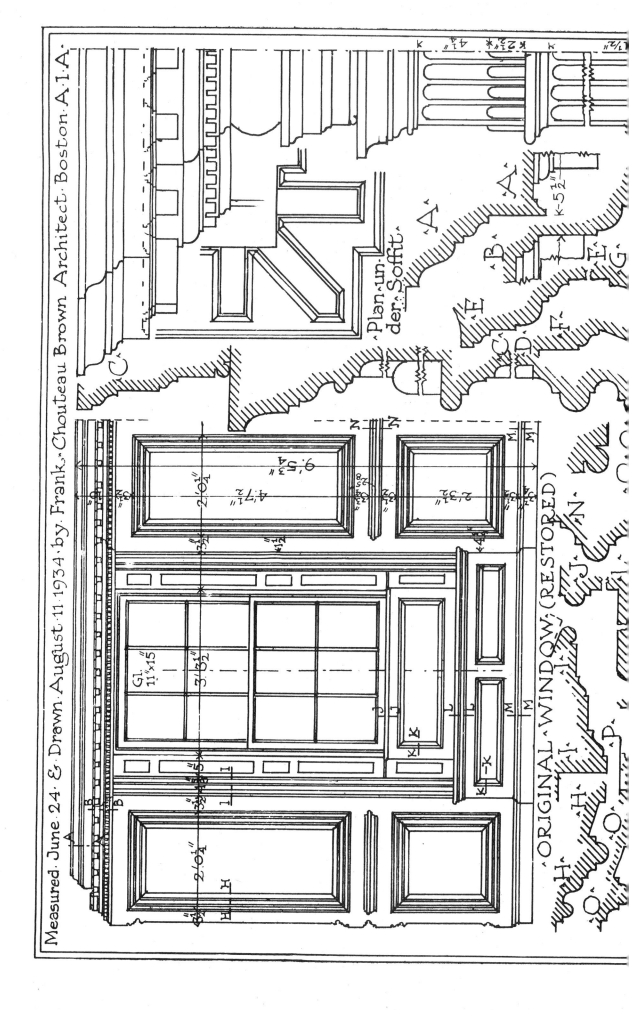

Measured·June·24·&·Drawn·August·11·1934·by·Frank·Chouteau·Brown·Architect·Boston·A.I.A.

ORIGINAL·WINDOW·(RESTORED)

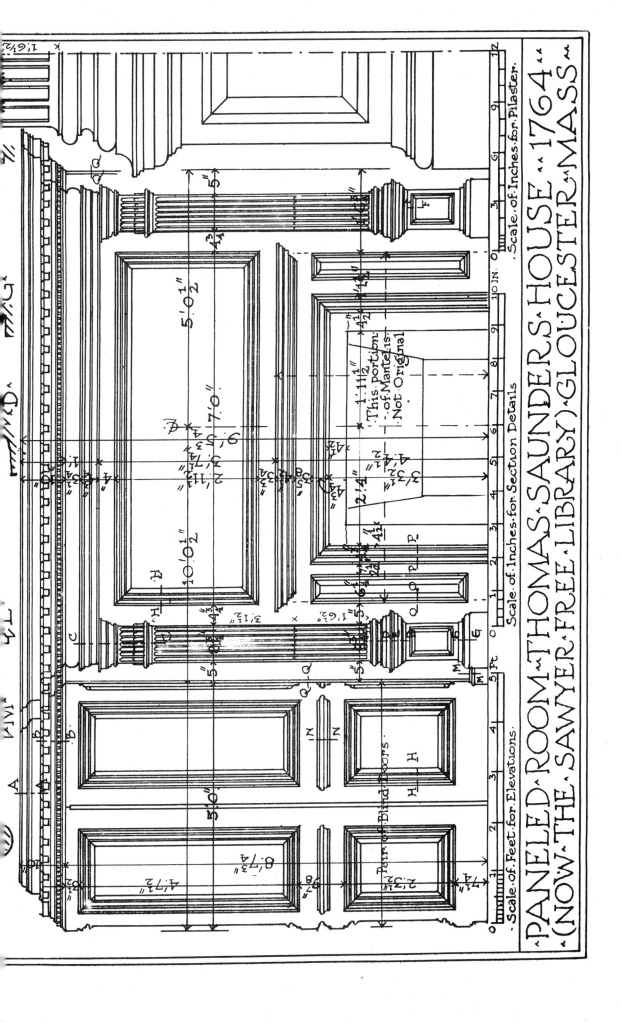

PANELED·ROOM·THOMAS·SAUNDERS·HOUSE·"1764"
·(NOW·THE·SAWYER·FREE·LIBRARY)·GLOUCESTER·MASS·

·Scale·of·Feet·for·Elevations·

Scale·of·Inches·for·Section·Details·

·Scale·of·Inches·for·Pilaster·

This·portion·
·of·Mantel·is·
·Not·Original·

·Pair·of·Blind·Doors·

The Dining Room
THE BABSON HOUSE—1740—GLOUCESTER, CAPE ANN, MASSACHUSETTS

THE BABSON HOUSE—1740—GLOUCESTER, CAPE ANN, MASSACHUSETTS

THE SAUNDERS HOUSE—1764-

THE MACKENZIE HOUSE—1760—90 MIDDLE STREET, GLOUCESTER, MASSACHUSETTS

"OLD COLLINS HOUSE"—1760-70—254 MAIN STREET, GLOUCESTER, MASSACHUSETTS

PANELED ROOM IN "OLD COLLINS HOUSE"—1760-70—GLOUCESTER, CAPE ANN, MASSACHUSETTS

THE DENNISON HOUSE—1727—SANDY BAY ROAD, ANNISQUAM, MASSACHUSETTS

Annisquam, Massachusetts

As soon as a fully framed structure was attempted it was natural that the New England settlers should turn to the mediæval type of timber-framed dwelling, with which they had been familiar at home, as a model for their construction in this new country. Consequently, the heavy sill-and-cornerpost frame, with plate and girt mortised and held with oak pins, came naturally into use. When, as at first, beaten earth was used as the floor, the sill was merely laid upon this base, or a few flat stones were placed at the corners or along the length for better support. The "raised sills" showing above the floor levels in a few houses (no less than four such may still be seen about Cape Ann) are a survival from this very time.

These framed structural outlines were then boarded upon the outside, usually with inch or inch-and-a-quarter thick boards, running perpendicularly from sill to plate or gable rafter ends; and pinned or nailed to the larger horizontal timbers, with small studdings used only to frame around a door or window opening. Sometimes these boards were tongued and grooved and molded at the edges; sometimes they were merely set close together and the spaces between filled with mud or clay, lime mortar or plaster.

The one-story house has often only one or two rooms upon the lower floor with an attic overhead, frequently left undivided. (Indeed, it is usually still found in this latter condition in many cottages along the coast, or inland in the country, built from a hundred to a hundred and fifty years ago!) At first access to this attic was by scuttle and ladder; replaced a little later by a steep stair running sharply up from beside the "Hall," or in the front entry.

The chimney was the most important part of these early houses. Built of stone or brick, set in mud or lime shell mortar, it was usually located at one end of these simpler types of dwellings, which were then most naturally enlarged by adding another room or two beyond the chimney, thus at once obtaining access to it and doubling the house in length. The next enlargement usually took the form of a long rear "leanto"; with possible other later additions developing as end "ells" or further "leantos" increasing the length of the structure, sometimes to a very considerable extent.

Possibly the favorite means of enlarging the early houses, however, was by leaving the older portion, nearly undisturbed, to serve as a kitchen ell; and adding a new—and very much larger house—usually at one or the other end. Sometimes this was done, as in the Riggs house here shown, by continuing the new part in length along the same frontage as the old, which almost invariably faced to the south. Sometimes it was added either at an angle, or quite at right angles to the older structure, the new front then often being to the east or west. This later method was perhaps often adopted from the fact that it was by this means possible to face the house anew upon the road; which had probably been built long after the original cottage had been informally placed facing south across some pleasant pasture, or looking out upon some livelier water view.

Thomas Riggs, "scrivener," the second Town Clerk of Gloucester and its first Schoolmaster, settled on Cape Ann at "Goose Cove," in 1658, and built the pitch-roof portion of the present dwelling of squared pine logs 15 inches thick, probably shortly previous to the year 1660. The "gambrel" part was added by a grandson, George Riggs, about 1700. This dwelling still stands in Vine Street, near the Riverdale Willows, only a short distance beyond "Church Green," which is just north and at the back of the well known White-Ellery House, generally dated as 1703 or 4, but probably built nearer 1710. This was the parsonage of the first minister, Rev. John White, of the Parish Church that stood across the Green. From 1738 onward it was used as a Tavern, or Ordinary, by James Stevens and his successors. One of the first houses in the Massachusetts Bay Colony (though not actually erected on Cape Ann) was the Community House, the materials for which were brought over from England. It stood just across on the mainland, in that part of Gloucester known as "Stage Fort Park"; and was afterwards removed and re-erected in Naumkeag, now Salem.

Another early house nearby was built for the home

THE RIGGS HOUSE—1660-1700—RIVERDALE, CAPE ANN, MASSACHUSETTS

Fireplace

THE RIGGS HOUSE

THE ROBINSON HOMESTEAD—1710-15—LANESVILLE, MASSACHUSETTS

THE WHITE-ELLERY HOUSE—1703-10—GLOUCESTER, MASSACHUSETTS

FRAMED STAIRCASE *Second Flight*   *First Flight*

THE DENNISON HOUSE—1727—SANDY BAY ROAD, ANNISQUAM, MASSACHUSETTS

PANELED ROOM END, SECOND STORY

of Richard Dike or Dyke. A date as early as 1643 has been claimed for this dwelling; but it was more probably built much nearer 1668, at which time this property—with a dwelling upon it—was transferred to John Fitch. It was again sold in 1714 to John Colt; and the pleasantly proportioned paneling of the principal room, and the stairway, are probably both from this or an even later date.

Most of the historical background of the early years of Cape Ann best relate to the history of its largest city, Gloucester. But those who know it only for that picturesque, overbuilt area surrounding the irregular shores of its busy Harbor; or for the summer reaches of its rocky moorlands from Eastern Point through Bass Rocks to Land's End; or even the teeming artist colonies of Rockport and Bearskin Neck, can know little or nothing of old Annisquam, oldest settlement of all the Cape. And indeed, few do know much about this sleepy little settlement, stretched out along the landlocked waters of "the Cove." The casual sight-seer, touring around the Cape, passes it entirely by; as does also the usual summer sojourner, going back and forth between the summer colonies fronting westerly across Ipswich Bay and the stations at Gloucester or Rockport. To feel its old-world charm one must turn aside from the main highway, down a narrow lane coming out upon the "floating bridge" that crosses the mouth of the Cove, or if coming from Bay View, swing sharply right back of the church at its innermost tip, so continuing along the narrow winding Leonard Street, from which circuitous lanes lead backward and forward, bending around rock out-crops, old stone benches and huge butternut trees to connect with backyards of places fronting the water-way, or reach the much-used side doors of houses whose fronts overhang other inner yards, or overlook low-lying roofs to the far wind-blown stretches of Winnegoeschieke—formerly Coffin's—Beach.

Embowered in the long untrimmed verdure of thick hedges, or heavily limbed low-hanging trees, many an old house lies quietly sleeping and hidden, a mere gravel-toss from a practicable street; that may nevertheless end unexpectedly—and somewhat sud-denly—at the water's edge; or against a heavy sea wall; or merely die out of existence between two or three old fenced yards and as many angularly slop-ing cottages, helter-skelterly faced to any and all points of the boxable compass.

On this limited, and irregular area, between 1631 and 1633, a few men and families from Plymouth effected the first permanent settlement on Cape Ann. Meanwhile the fishing at Gloucester was being estab-lished and that town was finally incorporated in 1642. The same year, according to early records, a building "boom" was the cause of setting up a sawmill at River-dale, which was about midway between Annisquam and Gloucester. Aided by the output of this mill, the second generation of settlers covered their early squared log houses with clapboards, laid sawed board floors, and applied split shingles over end wall boarding and on roof scantlings.

The first permanent settlers at Annisquam were made into the Third Parish in 1728, while the third meeting house of the First Parish had been raised on "Meeting House Green" in May of 1700, being de-scribed as "a building 40 by 40, with 16-foot posts, plastered with lime and hair," and costing £253.

Meanwhile the early simpler square little houses, scattered about Riverdale and Annisquam, were being lengthened and enlarged, "raised" to an added story height; and soon—near the end of the Seventeenth Century—a few four-room, full two-story houses were being built. Along the shores of "the Cove" old single houses with huge chimney at one end were also being lengthened by building another dwelling upon the outer side of the chimney, originally per-haps to house a younger generation of the same family; later to pass by marriage into quite alien hands. A number of old examples of this stand about the Cape, one being what is now known as "The Castle," built shortly after 1700 upon the bank of the Cove, with a huge chimney top only to mark its age from the pass-ing roadway, though from the water it may be seen to better advantage.

Nearby is the house built almost as early, the home of Madame Goss, used as officers' quarters in the War

COTTAGE
AT HEAD
OF COVE—
ABOUT 1700—
ANNISQUAM,
MASSACHUSETTS

THE
HARRADEN
HOUSE
—1657—
ANNISQUAM,
MASSACHUSETTS

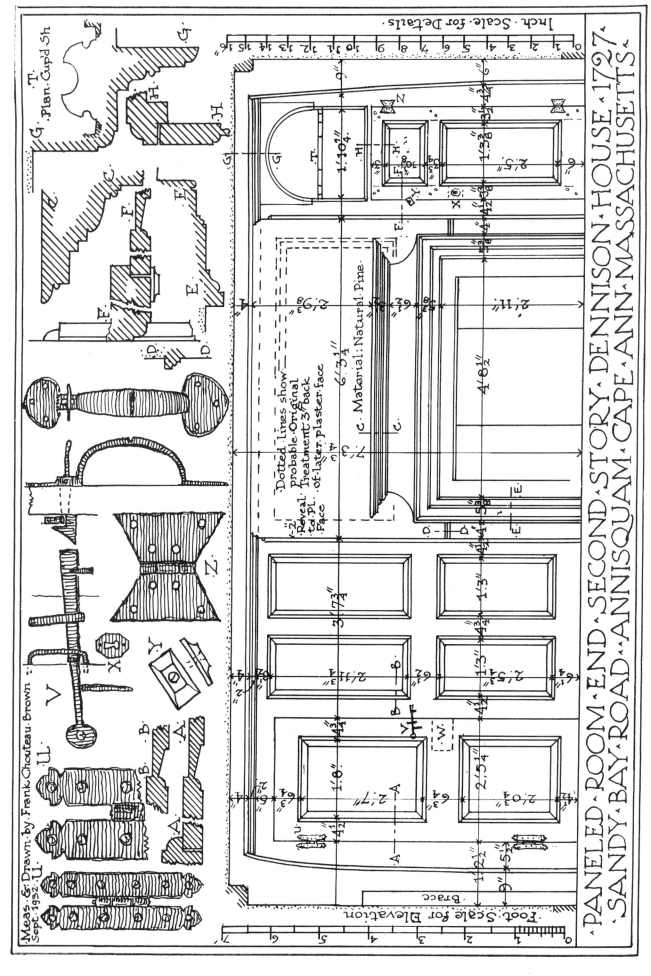

· PANELED · ROOM · END · SECOND · STORY · DENNISON · HOUSE · 1727 ·
· SANDY · BAY · ROAD · ANNISQUAM · CAPE · ANN · MASSACHUSETTS ·

Meas. & Drawn. by. Frank. Chouteau. Brown.
Sept. 1932.

Foot. Scale. for. Elevation.

Inch. Scale. for. Details.

Dotted. lines. show
probable. Original
Treatment 3" back
of. later. plaster. face

2" Reveal. to. Pl.
Face

C. Material: Natural. Pine.

Brace

174

THE DYKE-WHEELER HOUSE—ABOUT 1668—GLOUCESTER, MASSACHUSETTS

of 1812, but now hopelessly changed upon the outside; as is also the case with the Old Tavern, built just before 1700, and used as a soldiers' barracks in 1812. This still stands across the street from the Harraden house. The latter, with its earliest portion built about 1657 for Edward Harraden, one of the first settlers, has since been much changed about, added to, and built over, having now two "leantos," of different levels, a one- and a two-story section, at the rear.

Continuing along the main street, passing the village center store and post office, and many cottages of age and charm, the little house on the corner of Arlington Street that is reproduced may be seen—and, almost at the Cove's end, the little gambrel house, built probably soon after 1700, that is perhaps the most perfect of all the remaining cottages of modest appeal and venerable age now to be found upon the Cape.

At the "Head of the Cove" stands the old Church. Although the present building dates only from 1831, its predecessor was planted there in 1728!—surrounded with a pleasant group of little cottages and one more pretentious house of about 1800 (of all of which more will be heard anon), while nearly across the main roadway, leading up into the interior of the Cape, is the old "Sandy Bay Road," now Revere St., leading up to the old quarries and one end of "Dog Town Common" (and that, too, is another story!).

In a pleasant valley among the woods, at what appears to be the very end of the road, lies the old Dennison House, dating from 1727, though following precisely a much earlier style. Although but

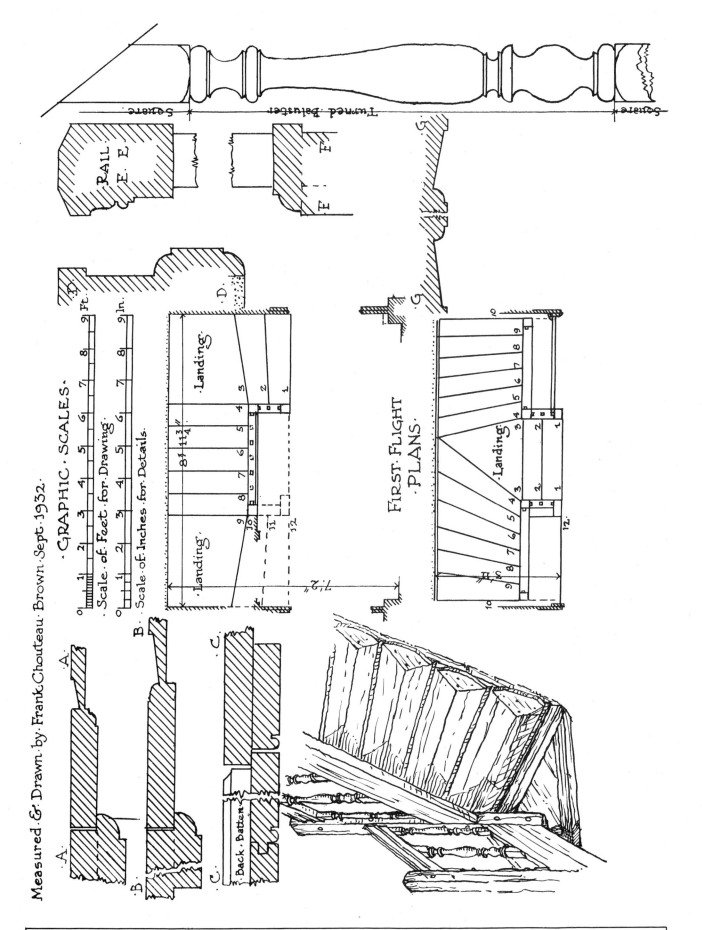

Square Turned Baluster Square

RAIL E E

F F

E E

G

G

Landing

8¾ 11¾"

7' 2"

Landing

Landing

FIRST FLIGHT PLANS

Landing

Measured & Drawn by Frank Chouteau Brown Sept 1932.

·GRAPHIC·SCALES·

Ft.

Scale of Feet for Drawing.

In.

B. Scale of Inches for Details.

A.

A

B.

B

C.

Back Batten

C

·PINE·FRAMED·STAIRCASE·IN·OLD·DENNISON·HOUSE·1727·
·SANDY·BAY·ROAD·ANNISQUAM·CAPE·ANN·MASSACHUSETTS·

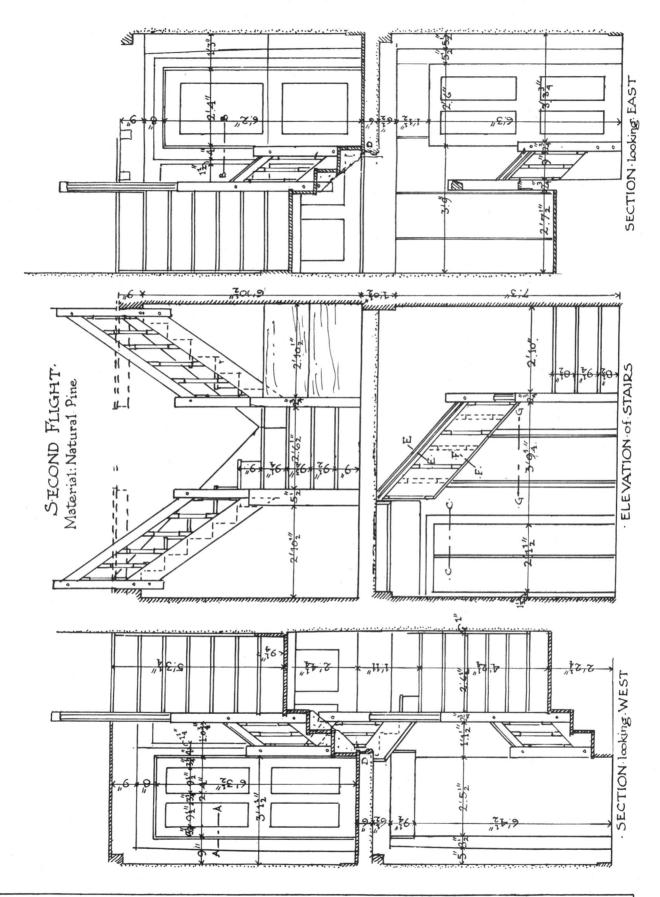

SECTION · looking · EAST

SECOND FLIGHT.
Material: Natural Pine

· ELEVATION · of · STAIRS

SECTION · looking · WEST

· PINE · FRAMED · STAIRCASE · IN · OLD · DENNISON · HOUSE · 1727 ·
· SANDY · BAY · ROAD · ANNISQUAM · CAPE · ANN · MASSACHUSETTS ·

HOUSE AT CORNER OF ARLINGTON STREET, ANNISQUAM, MASSACHUSETTS

little known, the place has very recently come into the possession of Mr. Earl Sanborn, who is transferring his Glass Studio to a new structure built in back of the old dwelling, where windows for the new Washington Cathedral are now taking shape.

As yet no attempt has been made to reconstruct or restore the original aspect of the house, or its interiors. Outside, its age is still disguised under a comparatively modern coating of shingles; and every here or there in the interior still appear evidences of the individuality of some previous owner or tenant. Nevertheless, the views taken show a more than usually interesting staircase, carrying out in natural pine almost exactly the forms of its oak predecessors of fifty years before; the balusters alone, while still of even the earliest outlines, marking the difference. The

details of this stairway, as well as its open support underneath, may be studied also in a measured drawing; another sheet shows some of the panelled ends remaining in the rooms. One of these, showing the natural pine,, in a bedroom, has also been photographed; with a later, but still finely appealing mantel; and a charming original cupboard. Other panelling has been painted over, and some of the fireplaces filled up, or reduced in size; while the old "Hall" contains an example of a mantelshelf that, if not "an original" in date, may have been added soon after, from its simple appropriateness and feeling for relation to the room and its panelling.

Despite its later date, this house is among the earliest in appearance of the few full two-story dwellings on the Cape; and has the earliest type of staircase.

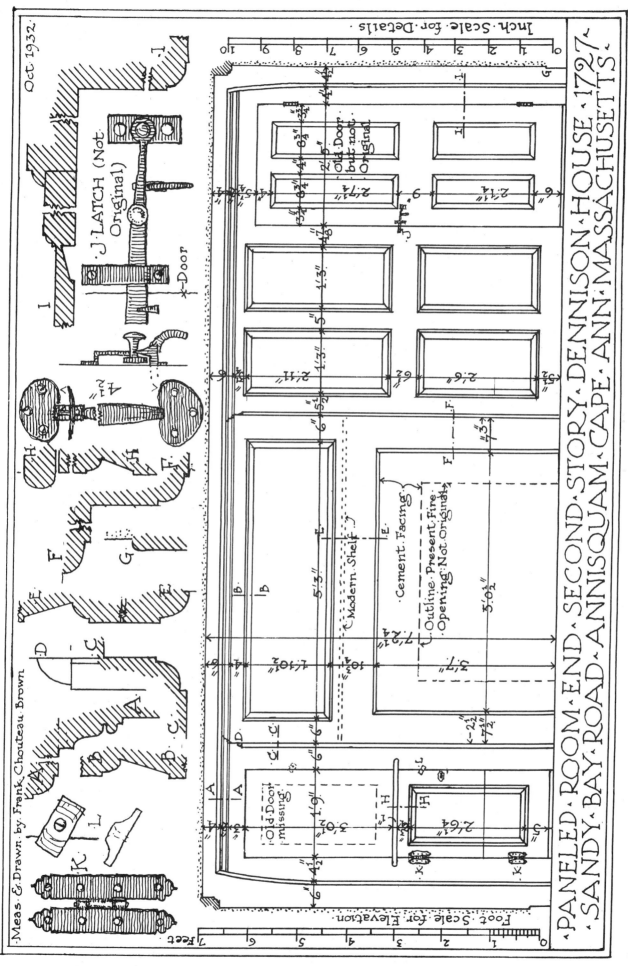

Meas. & Drawn by Frank Chouteau Brown

Oct 1932.

Inch Scale for Details.

J LATCH (Not Original)

Door

Old Door but not Original

Old Door missing

Modern Shelf

Cement Facing

Outline Present Fire Opening Not Original

Foot Scale for Elevation.

PANELED ROOM END SECOND STORY DENNISON HOUSE 1727
SANDY BAY ROAD ANNISQUAM CAPE ANN MASSACHUSETTS.

ENTRANCE HALL AND STAIRCASE
SARAH ORNE JEWETT HOUSE—SOUTH BERWICK, MAINE
BUILT BY JOHN HAGGINS IN 1774

New England Entrance Halls and Stairways

T HE ENTRANCE hallway was a refinement in living to which most of the early emigrants to the New World had been unaccustomed in their own homeland. Those leaving the south of England had previously been living in survivals from mediæval culture, principally in the farmsteads and village cottages, of which many picturesque examples have survived to the present day. Their picturesqueness, however, did not provide even the elemental comforts and conveniences to which every individual believes himself entitled today. Even the smaller Manor House plan did not always provide any Hall, and when it did it took then the form rather of a general living space than any area intended only for circulation and privacy in connecting the various residential elements of the family menage. In Louis XIV's palace at Versailles, the further bedrooms could only be reached by passing through all those between.

In 1600 the mass of English architecture was of Tudor or earlier date. It was to be a dozen or more years before Inigo Jones returned from Italy, with his 1601 edition of Palladio crowded with his own marginal annotations; and a good many more years were to elapse before the newer style of open plan was to become familiar, even to the wealthier and more sycophantic courtiers of Henry VIII and Elizabeth; and more years still before it began to affect in the slightest the types of common dwellings with which those who first settled the Massachusetts Bay Colony were familiar. Along our southern coast, to be sure, the plans and appearance of the larger houses began much earlier to disclose that they were in some small

part expressive of the new fashions in the amenities of living that were permeating the newer and better dwellings of England.

Neither did the English climate require much shelter for these cottage dwellers, save from the rain; consequently, the outer entrance door usually opened directly into one end of the general living, eating, and cooking room of the small cottage. It was this one general room that the earliest homes in New England first reproduced, with a large fireplace for cooking and heating. A large scullery opening off this room and another space to provide warm sleeping quarters for the family were the first additions. The space under the roof long remained an undivided attic for the sleeping quarters of children or servants, almost to the present century, and many examples are still to be found in outer New England.

But the rigorous climate of the northern colonies soon forced the settlers to adopt different details of arrangement than they had found livable in the Tudor dwellings of old England. So, to protect the occupants of the "Hall" or "Fire Room" from drafts when the entrance door was opened, this was removed behind the corner of the large fireplace with an inner partition and door to make a "vestibule," out of the other side of which a ladder or steep winding stair—which otherwise might be placed in one corner of the "Fire Room"—might rise to the low attic story above.

As the houses became more definitely two-story-and-attic structures, the Hall and stairway increased in size and importance; a development that became even more definite when the plan increased to four rooms upon each floor.

The staircase now had usually two instead of the earlier three runs, and the first was made much the longer, in order to obtain headroom, usually for passage purposes to o t h e r parts of the house plan, under the cross landing or last run at the rear end of the open Hall. Among the most dignified of these presentations w a s the Entrance H a l l with underarch, and main cross landing with its Palladian window - door opening at that level onto the rear staircase, which was the one that then continued to the third story, leaving the main staircase to end upon the s e c o n d story level and so connect only with the principal front second story rooms. A fine example of this arrangement was in t h e Benjamin Hall, Jr., House, at

ENTRANCE HALL, ARCHWAY, AND STAIRCASE
COL. ISAAC ROYALL HOUSE—c.1733—MEDFORD

Medford: o n e of t h r e e Hall family houses existing since 1785, side by side, until the summer of 1938, when this particular building succumbed to commercial pressure and was demolished!

That varied decorative treatments of this landing doorway connecting the front and rear halls were frequently found in Massachusetts, is indicated by the two other examples, both from Salem.

Of course, this is merely another expression of the graceful and impressive arched window motive, that often appears in the rear house wall, to open on the main staircase hall landing, as in the Jeremiah Lee Mansion, 1768, in Marblehead.

With the fully-developed two-room-deep long Entrance Hallway a large

ENTRANCE HALL—SHOWING CROSSBEAM AND STAIRCASE
TOBIAS LEAR HOUSE—c.1740—PORTSMOUTH, NEW HAMPSHIRE

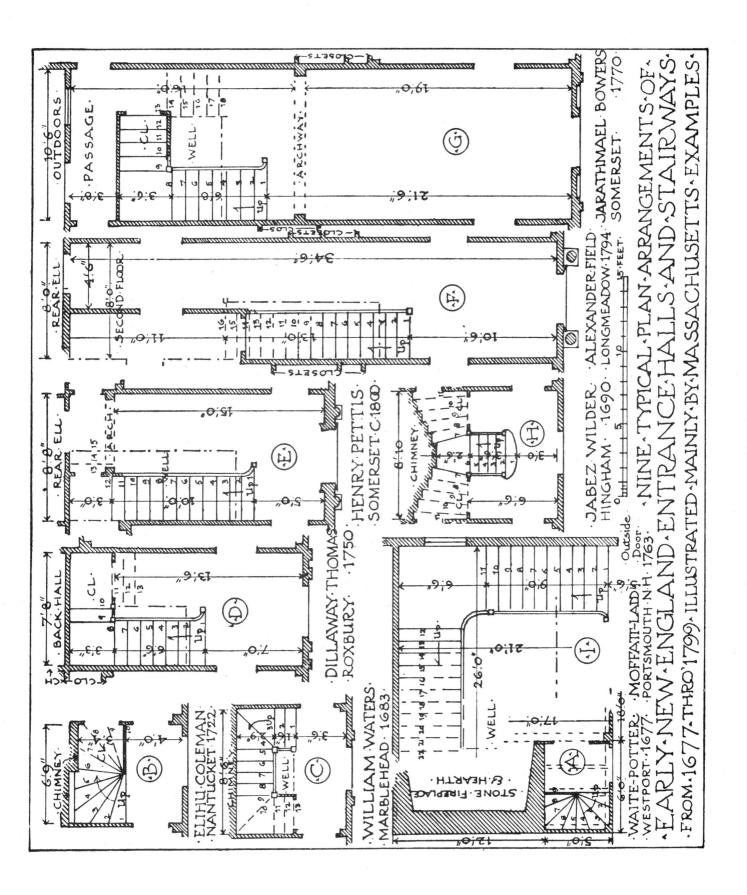

NINE·TYPICAL·PLAN·ARRANGEMENTS·OF·
EARLY·NEW·ENGLAND·ENTRANCE·HALLS·AND·STAIRWAYS·
FROM·1677·THRO'1799·ILLUSTRATED·MAINLY·BY·MASSACHUSETTS·EXAMPLES·

·JARATHMAEL·BOWERS· ·SOMERSET· ·1770·

·ALEXANDER·FIELD· ·LONGMEADOW·1794·

·JABEZ·WILDER· ·HINGHAM· ·1690·

·HENRY·PETTIS· ·SOMERSET·C·1800·

·DILLAWAY·THOMAS· ·ROXBURY· ·1750·

·ELIHU·COLEMAN· ·NANTUCKET·1722·

·WILLIAM·WATERS· ·MARBLEHEAD· 1683·

·WAITE-POTTER· ·WESTPORT·1677·
·MOFFATT-LADD· ·PORTSMOUTH·N.H.·1763·

183

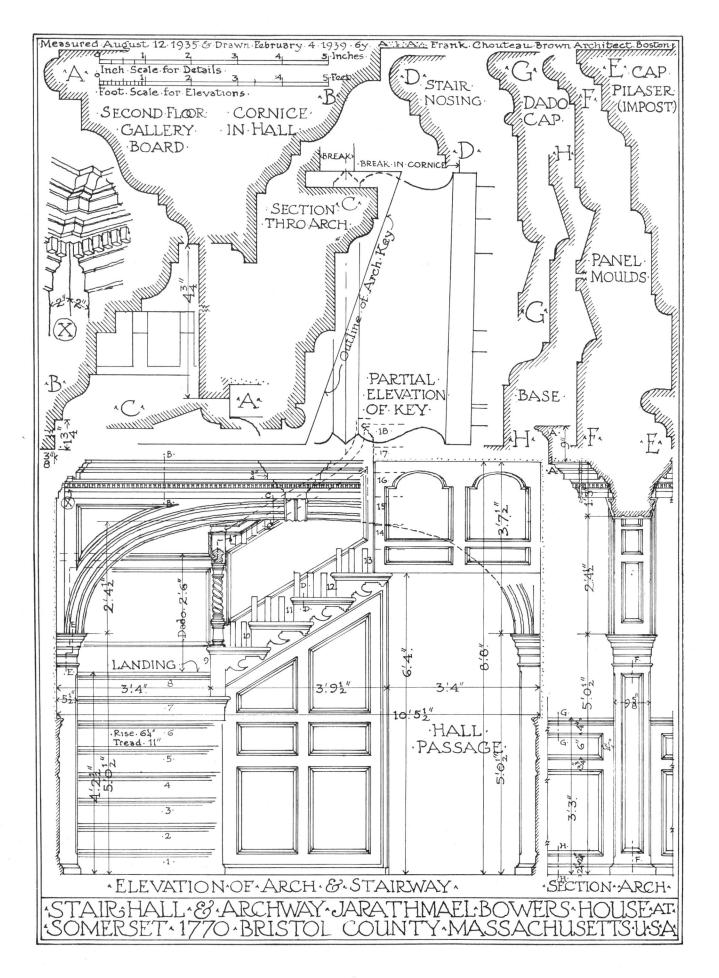

Measured August 12 1935 & Drawn February 4 1939 by A.I.A. Frank Chouteau Brown Architect Boston

A
Inch Scale for Details
Foot Scale for Elevations

SECOND FLOOR
GALLERY
BOARD

CORNICE
IN HALL

B

D STAIR
NOSING

G

E CAP
PILASER
(IMPOST)

F

DADO
CAP

H

SECTION
THRO ARCH
C

BREAK
BREAK IN CORNICE
D
D

Outline of Arch Key

PANEL
MOULDS

PARTIAL
ELEVATION
OF KEY

BASE

B
C
A

X

LANDING

Dado 2·6"

Rise 6¼"
Tread 11"

HALL
PASSAGE

ELEVATION OF ARCH & STAIRWAY

SECTION ARCH

STAIR HALL & ARCHWAY JARATHMAEL BOWERS HOUSE AT
SOMERSET 1770 BRISTOL COUNTY MASSACHUSETTS USA

184

crossing near the center of its length, and recessing the staircase within a further Hallway, makes its appearance. In its earliest form, it may be seen as a simple exposed structural girder, crossing the ceiling of the hall at this location, in the Tobias Lear House, c.1740, at Portsmouth, N. H. This is its simplest manifestation. In the region round about Portsmouth there are at least a dozen varied examples of the large Hall cross-archway, with a few others in

Vassall, in 1746, to the earlier house, built before 1686, by John Vassall in Cambridge with its individual use of an outlined bracket form, in place of a capital, over a very flat wall pilaster from above which the elliptical arch springs; and the somewhat similar arrangement in the Entrance Hallway of the Col. Isaac Royall House, c.1733, at Medford, where the bracket is more elaborate and the pilaster is given a bolder projection.

VIEW THROUGH ENTRANCE HALL ARCHWAY TOWARD STAIRCASE
JARATHMAEL BOWERS HOUSE—1770—SOMERSET, MASSACHUSETTS

Maine, in Massachusetts, and also in Rhode Island.

Accompanying examples are the Jewett House, 1774, in South Berwick, Me.; the Bowers House, 1770, in Somerset; the Captain Gregory Purcell ("John Paul Jones") House, 1757-59, in Portsmouth, N. H.; and the Nickels-Sortwell House, 1807-8, in Wiscasset, Maine. Two other examples near Boston are the cross-Hall arch in the portion added by Maj. Henry

A radically different and unusual plan is shown at H, from the Jabez Wilder Cottage, at Hingham, 1690. Here the staircase starts upward from just inside the entrance door and in the middle of the Hallway, with a flight which divides and rises at right and left against the receding face of the chimney, to end at the very doorways of the two rooms under its "rainbow" roof. Finally, at I, is the plan of a quite unusual *corner* Entrance Hall, as it appears in the Moffatt-Ladd House, 1763, at Portsmouth, N. H. The same plan is repeated, upon a somewhat smaller scale, in at least two other Portsmouth houses.

Despite the apparently elaborate layout of several of these Hall plans, all (with the possible exception of the one last named) nevertheless conform within a reasonably economical floor area, in relation to the space covered by the whole house. In the case of the

toward each other, to meet on a short landing near the center of the Hall's length, with a final short run of two or three steps at right angle, to the floor above.

Prime attention is given here to the Entrance Hall, rather than the staircase; yet the two are so closely associated in early New England house plans, that it is not possible to picture one without the other. That much more might be made of the Hallway is proven by the Azor Orne and Nickels-Sortwell en-

Courtesy Soc. Pres. N. E. Antiquities

Entrance Hall, Archway, and Staircase
CAPTAIN GREGORY PURCELL HOUSE—1757-59—PORTSMOUTH, NEW HAMPSHIRE

Nickels-Sortwell Hall, the effect of Entrance Hallway, cross arch, and staircase are all secured within the one-room house depth.

Finally, mention should be made of another arrangement of staircases, each starting from near the doors at front and back house walls, and running

trances; while in the Coleman-Hollister Hallway, no staircase appears until the center of the Hall is passed, when this charmingly delicate stairway comes into full view. With the exception of this example, and the stairway of the Nickels-Sortwell House, the elliptical or semi-circular stair plan.

VIEW ALONG ENTRANCE HALL TOWARD REAR DOOR
SQUIRE WILLIAM SEVER HOUSE—1760—KINGSTON, MASS.

HALL AND ARCHWAY, LOOKING TOWARD GARDEN DOOR
MERRIMAN HOUSE—c.1820—BRISTOL, RHODE ISLAND

BENJAMIN HALL, JR., HOUSE—1785—MEDFORD, MASSACHUSETTS

JOSHUA WARD HOUSE—c.1765—SALEM, MASSACHUSETTS

ASSEMBLY HOUSE—1782—SALEM, MASSACHUSETTS

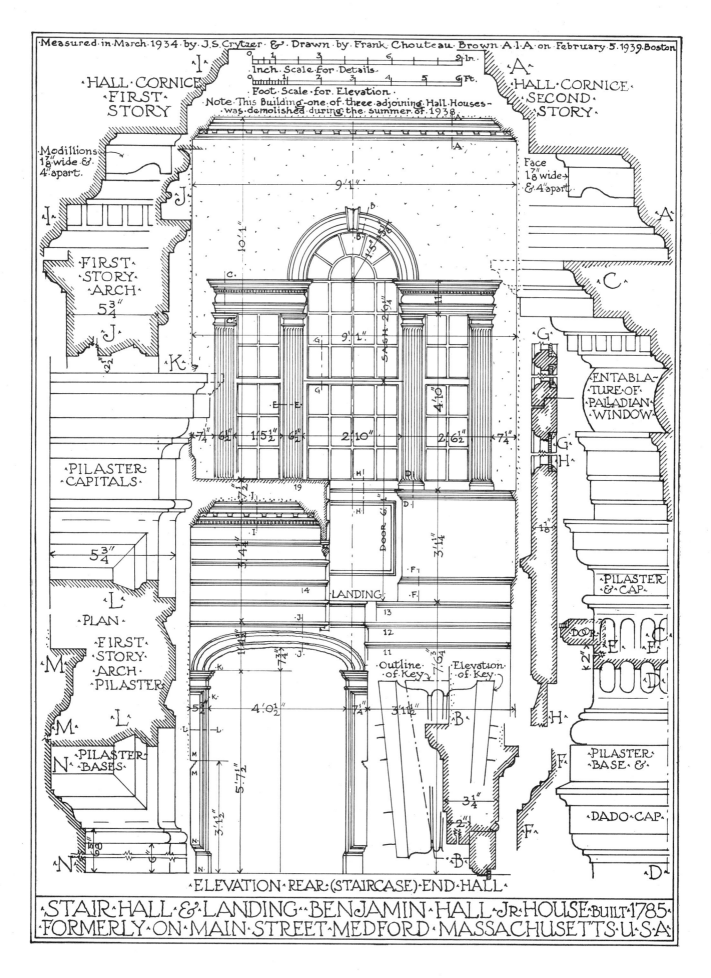

Measured in March 1934 by J.S.Crytzer & Drawn by Frank Chouteau Brown A.I.A on February 5.1939.Boston

Inch Scale for Details.

Foot Scale for Elevation

Note This Building one of three adjoining Hall Houses was demolished during the summer of 1938.

·HALL·CORNICE· ·FIRST· STORY

·HALL·CORNICE· ·SECOND· STORY

Modillions 1⅞" wide & 4" apart.

Face 1⅞" wide & 4" apart.

·FIRST· ·STORY· ·ARCH· 5¾"

·ENTABLA- TURE·OF· ·PALLADIAN· WINDOW·

·PILASTER· ·CAPITALS·

·PILASTER· ·& CAP·

·PLAN·

·FIRST· ·STORY· ·ARCH· ·PILASTER·

·PILASTER· ·BASES·

·PILASTER· ·BASE & ·

·DADO·CAP·

·Outline· ·of Key·

·Elevation· ·of Key·

·LANDING·

·ELEVATION· REAR· (STAIRCASE) END· HALL·

·STAIR·HALL·&·LANDING··BENJAMIN·HALL·Jr·HOUSE·BUILT·1785· FORMERLY·ON·MAIN·STREET·MEDFORD·MASSACHUSETTS·U·S·A·

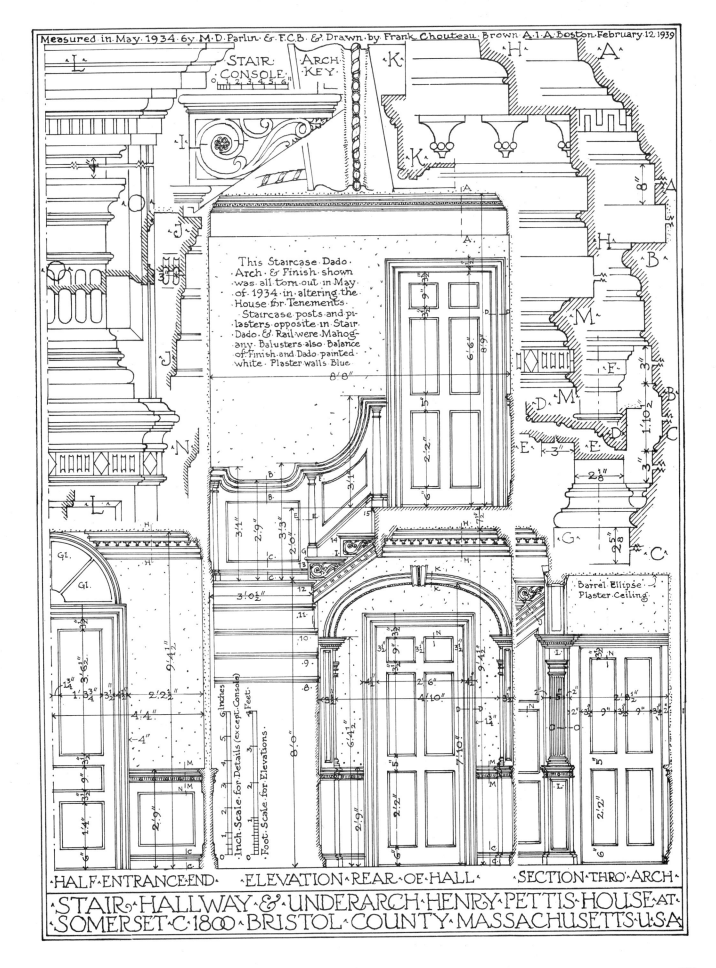

STAIR CONSOLE

ARCH KEY

This Staircase Dado Arch & Finish shown was all torn out in May of 1934 in altering the House for Tenements. Staircase posts and pilasters opposite in Stair Dado & Rail were Mahogany. Balusters also Balance of Finish and Dado painted white. Plaster walls Blue.

Barrel Ellipse Plaster Ceiling

Inch Scale for Details (except Console)

Foot Scale for Elevations

·HALF·ENTRANCE·END·   ·ELEVATION·REAR·OE·HALL·   ·SECTION·THRO·ARCH·

STAIR·HALLWAY·&·UNDERARCH·HENRY·PETTIS·HOUSE·AT·
SOMERSET·C·1800·BRISTOL·COUNTY·MASSACHUSETTS·U·S·A·

191

ENTRANCE HALL AND STAIRCASE
MOFFATT-LADD HOUSE—1763—PORTSMOUTH, NEW HAMPSHIRE

HALLWAY LOOKING TOWARD FRONT ENTRANCE
COLEMAN-HOLLISTER HOUSE—1796—GREENFIELD, MASSACHUSETTS

SEMI-CIRCULAR STAIRCASE IN RECESS OFF ENTRANCE HALL
COLEMAN-HOLLISTER HOUSE—1796—GREENFIELD, MASSACHUSETTS
ASHER BENJAMIN, ARCHITECT

JEREMIAH LEE MANSION—1768—MARBLEHEAD, MASSACHUSETTS

BALUSTERS 1"×⅝"

BALUSTERS ⅝"×1"

SCALE·FOR·D
1½"=1'-

GENERAL·PLAN
SCALE ⅛"=1'-0"

2ND FLOOR DOWN 20

FIRST FLOOR UP 20

New England Staircases

When the first Colonial dwellings began to attain the dignity of a full second story, with rooms of useable height, the temporary ladder-like arrangement that had previously served to reach the upper floor changed to a more permanent and a more ornamental feature in the American home. Sometimes it ran directly between partitions of wide board sheathing or plaster or, starting with a quarter wind at the bottom, it went steeply upward to the low chambers overhead. Or it reversed this process, starting straight up from beside the Kitchen in the "linter" (or "lean-to"), attaining the floor above with a quarter turn to right or left, as the case might be.

When the location against the front of a large chimney serving two end rooms, and possibly also a third at the rear, became common, the latter stair plan was soon changed to a flight of three runs—as in the Waters House at Marblehead—with either landings or winders at the corner angles, depending upon the height to be gained and the width of the chimney itself. Usually the chimney was spacious enough to permit of the landing (as in the Salmon Falls staircase), thus making the stairs easier to take by means of the brief "breather" at the turn, breaking up the steepness of the runs, generally of three to five risers each. And this remained the favorite stair arrangement, until the chimneys were removed to the outer end walls or placed midway between a pair of end rooms, when the Hall might be run entirely through the house from front to back, with a long straight flight of stairs, sometimes with a turn at top or bottom.

The staircase of the old-time New England house is always one of its most attractive adjuncts. No matter how simple, its proportions are almost invariably good and it is generally regarded as a most attractive feature of the early Colonial structure. Even the crudest and most primitive examples are today accepted as interesting exhibits of the inherent feeling of their builders for the design appropriate to its environment and the method of construction that was most perfectly adapted to express the materials available.

In the earliest existing houses, where the stairs are still to be seen in something approaching their original condition, built perhaps during the last half of the Seventeenth Century, the staircases usually had no baluster of any kind. It was then customary to extend the simple boarded face of the partition under the stair run up to the height of a low rail or to the level of the second story floor above, thus stiffening the stair construction and simplifying the problem of protecting the stair edge.

When the boarding—usually at that time some variation of the feather-edge pattern—did not extend up to the second floor timbering, it sometimes stopped at a height of two feet to thirty inches above the step rise, and was capped with a narrow moulded crown strip, with a small bedmoulding upon the face, or upon both sides. Or it might merely extend from the first floor to the stair stringer and a single piece of hand railing carried between simple rough posts at top and bottom, with the space below left open—as was probably the original condition of the Dr. Peaslee stairway in the brick Garrison House at Rock Village, Massachusetts, dating from 1675.

WARNER HOUSE STAIRCASE
—1718-22—PORTSMOUTH, N. H.

Of course, at that time, the entire stair construction was suspended from two "buttresses" or "raised stringers," one on each side of the steps, into which the risers and treads were housed. Again, with this form of design, and either one or two sloping rails pinned at each end into the upright posts at landing and floor levels, this treatment served as a sort of structural "truss," obviously stiffening the carriage of the stairs, and suspending each flight from end to end, even with a turn or landing in between.

Most early staircases were so cramped that they were perforce carried around angles in the plan with a series of steps, making what is known as a "wind," rather than the pleasanter and easier "landing"—as in the King Hooper, Waters, rear Warner Stairs, and other numerous examples. And the angles of these winding steps are very generally not at the usual 22½, 30 or 45 degree, so regularly employed in modern stairbuilding, but some slight variation of these angles, the stair winders being usually "worked" or "handled" around the post, in the manner that appears in the plan of the Dennison staircase, and others here indicated.

Another detail characteristic of the early staircases is the informal variance of the height of the rail above tread and gallery level, being often higher than is the modern custom and, occasionally, much lower, while in those instances (as in the Wentworth Mansion at Salmon Falls) where the rail on each run of the flight is a handworked ramp made in one piece of material, it shows considerable extremes of height, as appears in the varied lengths of the balusters.

The old rule-of-thumb proportioning of stair-rise to stair-tread dimension—"that twice the rise added to the width of tread should equal 25 inches" (or, at least, come within the extremes of 24 to 26 inches)—has been pretty consistently adhered to in all old work.

The turned baluster was probably introduced some time between 1675 and 1700. At first wide-spaced and roughly turned or "whittled" out of soft wood (as in the Peaslee stairs at Rock Village) it was often — as there — inserted under older existing rails. Its turnings gradually became more ornate and elaborate—as in the Salmon Falls Mansion House, where a baluster pattern very advanced and delicate for its period, with an informal irregularity of turning that naively bespeaks its probable original date—until we reach the perfections obtained in the fine mahogany and workmanship of the spacious front stairs of the famed Jeremiah Lee Mansion at Marblehead, with its majestic width of seven feet!

It seems impossible that this fine workmanship was achieved by the inventive artisan, from a simple turning lathe. Yet the elaborate and delicately moulded posts and balusters of the Lee Mansion must have been achieved in 1768 with a common lathe, foot or water-powered. With this simple implement, geared to a slow even turning, a skilled workman could mark out these twists and spirals with the edge of his chisel, grooving them as deeply as he dared: and then, with their regularity once established, he could complete the grooving by hand, and finish off the twist at top or bottom by carving—as was always necessary, even with the most improved machines for this work, of which the earliest known in New England was not developed before 1860.

Or notice the skill and perfection of thoroughness with which the Dillaway House stairway has been worked out. This perfection may be contrasted with the Short House stairs, done in the advanced, comparatively rich and populous settlement of Newbury, and made for a far wealthier man than the simple parson who built the Dillaway House across the street from his Church on Eliot Square in Roxbury. For the Short House balusters, as magnified in their shadows on the wall, betray almost the extremes of variation, in their turnings and patterns, of any of the examples illustrated in this collection.

Some of these same variations are to be found in the earlier famed Warner House at Portsmouth, built between 1718 and 1722, at a cost of 10,000 pounds by one Capt. MacPhestris. But here probably other elements must be taken into account. Only the rear staircase now seems plausibly harmonious with its period. The front flight has been subjected to extensive alterations; probably the closed-in type of gallery treatment found on the landing and second floor expressing the older—and perhaps the original—design. The workmanship along the runs, and stair ends, dating from some later rebuilding or change—even though made soon after the dwelling was completed!

The Lee Mansion front stairs, with double twisted newel, three differently designed balusters on each tread, and its mahogany rail ramped at the stair well angles as well as at the landings, is among the most elaborate stair designs of the period. It also shows the characteristic wall dado, its cap following out the ramps and eases of the stair rail, but at a height some ten inches above the latter, that appears in all the best examples. Finally it also exhibits the boxed-in undercarriage, paneled upon the back face, that shows under the second run, extending from the landing to the second floor level.

PAUL WENTWORTH STAIRCASE
—1701—SALMON FALLS, N. H.

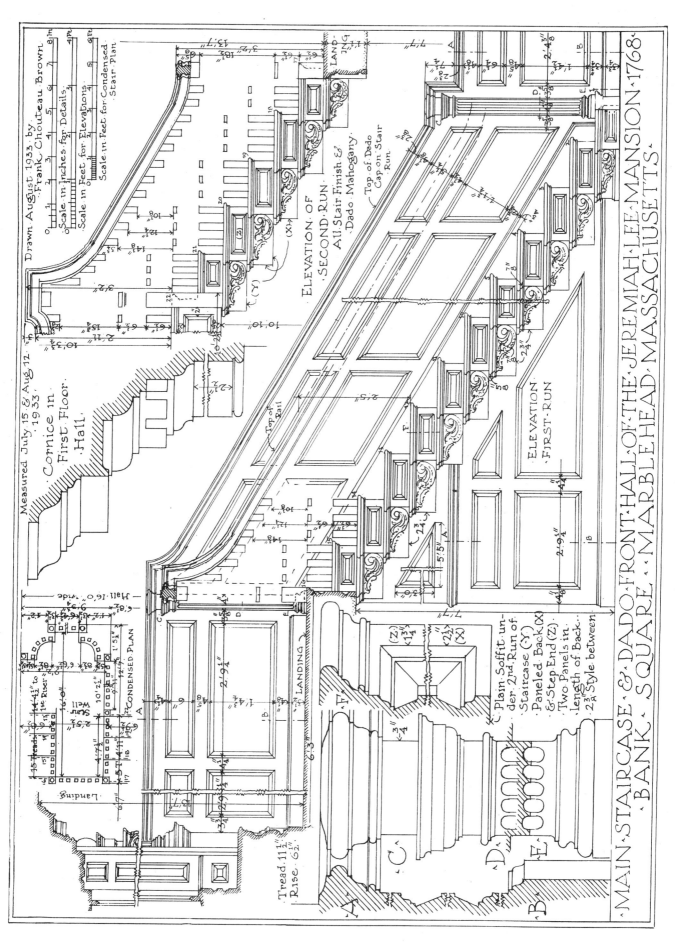

MAIN·STAIRCASE·&·DADO·FRONT·HALL·OF·THE·JEREMIAH·LEE·MANSION·1768·
·BANK·SQUARE·MARBLEHEAD·MASSACHUSETTS·

STAIR HALL—THE LEE MANSION—MARBLEHEAD, MASSACHUSETTS

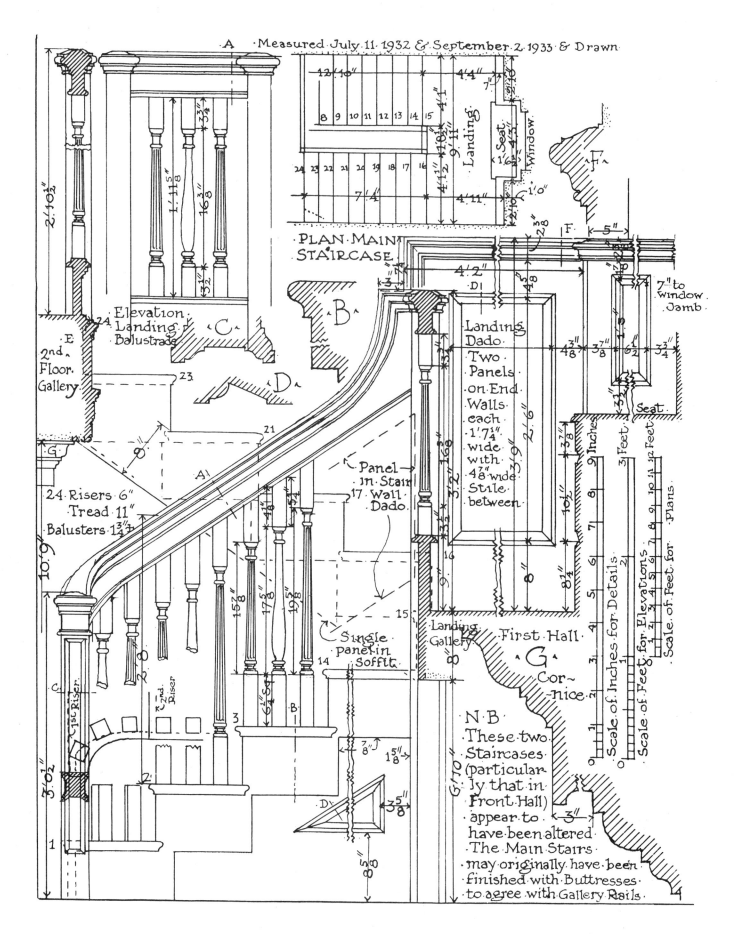

A Measured July 11 1932 & September 2 1933 & Drawn

PLAN MAIN
STAIRCASE

Elevation
Landing
Balustrade

E
2nd.
Floor.
Gallery

24 Risers 6"
Tread 11"
Balusters 13¾"

Panel
in Stair
Wall Dado.

Single
panel in
Soffit

Landing
Dado
Two
Panels
on End
Walls
each
1'7¼"
wide
with
4⅛" wide
Stile
between

Landing
Gallery

First Hall

G
Cor-
nice

7" to
Window
Jamb

Seat

Scale of Inches for Details

Scale of Feet for Elevations

Scale of Feet for Plans

N B
These two
Staircases
(particular-
ly that in
Front Hall)
appear to
have been altered
The Main Stairs
may originally have been
finished with Buttresses
to agree with Gallery Rails.

DETAILS·PRESENT·MAIN·STAIRCASE·
·BUILT·FOR·CAPT·MACPHESTRIS·AT

200

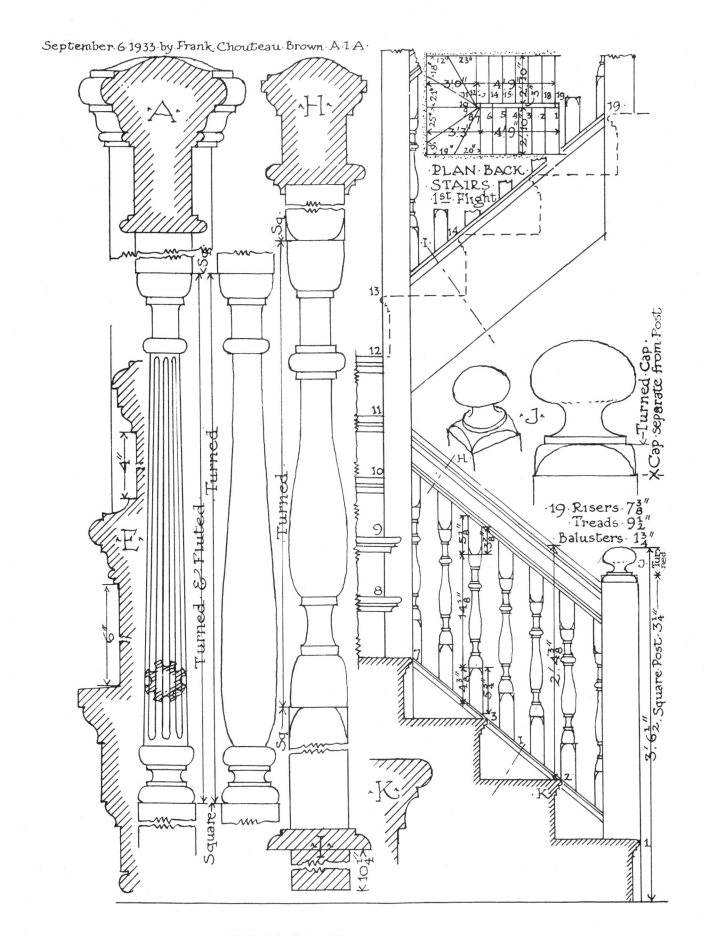

September 6 1933 by Frank Chouteau Brown A I A

·A·

·H·

Sq.

Turned

Turned & Fluted

Turned

·E·

4″

6″

Square

K 10¼

PLAN BACK
STAIRS
1st Flight

19

13

12

11

10

9

8

14

I

·J·

·H·

Turned Cap
Cap separate from Post

19 Risers 7⅜″
Treads 9½″
Balusters 1¾″

5⅝

5⅜

14⅛″

4¾″

5¼″

2′4⅜″

·K·

·J·

Turned

Square Post 3¼

3′6½″

3′6½″ Square Post 3¼

·K·

2

1

·REAR·STAIRS·WARNER·HOUSE·1718·22·
PORTSMOUTH·NEW·HAMPSHIRE·

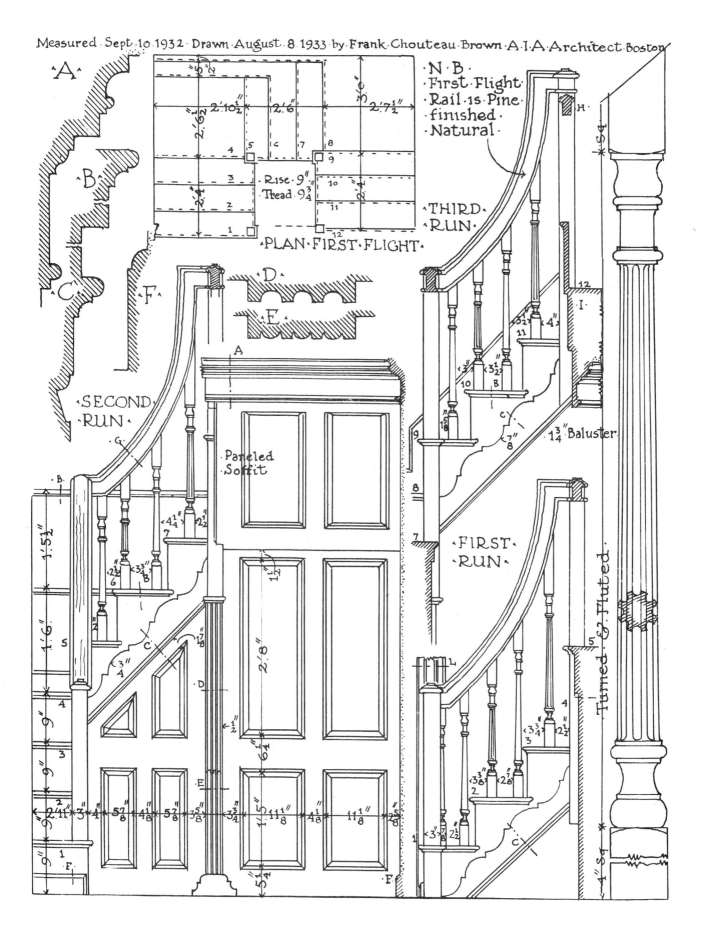

·A·

·B·

·C· ·F·

·D·

·E·

N·B·
First·Flight·
·Rail·is·Pine·
·finished·
·Natural·

·THIRD·
·RUN·

·PLAN·FIRST·FLIGHT·

Rise·9″·
Tread·9¾·

SECOND·
·RUN·

Paneled
·Soffit·

FIRST·
·RUN·

1¾″ Baluster·

Turned · & · Fluted ·

·MAIN·STAIRCASE·FIRST·TO·SECOND·
·COL·PAUL·WENTWORTH·MANSION·

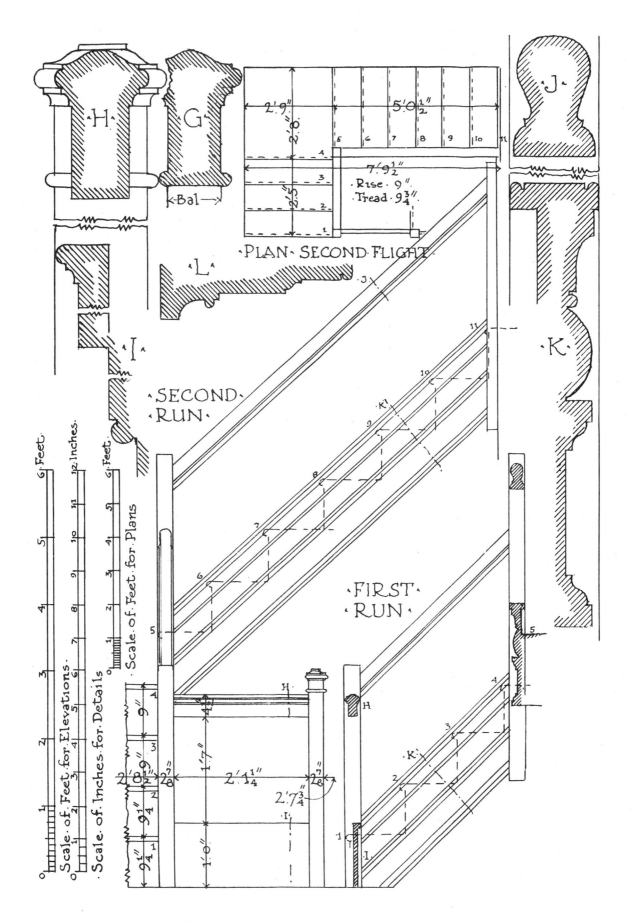

·H· ·G·

←Bal→

·L·

·I·

·SECOND· ·RUN·

2'9" 5'0½"

2'0"

2'5"

·PLAN· SECOND· FLIGHT·

7'9½"
·Rise· 9"
·Tread· 9¾"

·J·

·K·

·FIRST· ·RUN·

·Scale· of· Feet· for· Elevations.·
·Scale· of· Inches· for· Details·
·Scale· of· Feet· for· Plans·

6· Feet.
12· Inches.
6· Feet.

9"

1'7"

2'8" 8¾" 2⅞"

2'1¼"

2'7¾"

9¾"

9¼"

1'0"

H

2⅞"

2⅞"

·&· SECOND· TO· ATTIC· FLOORS·
1701· SALMON· FALLS· NEW· HAMPSHIRE·

203

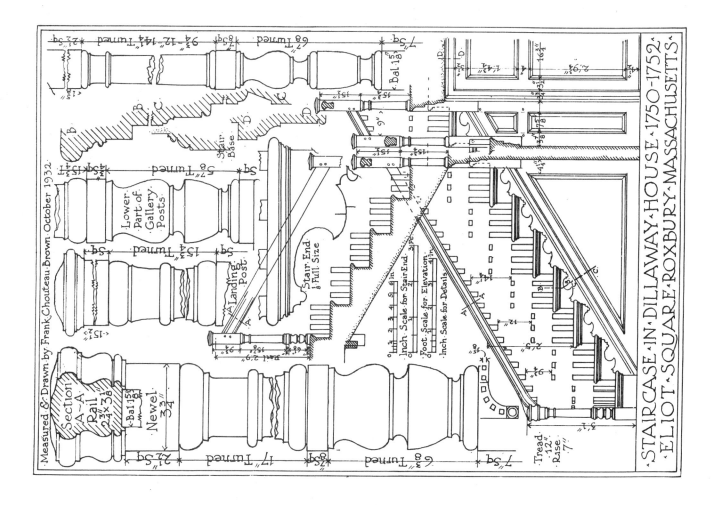

STAIRCASE·IN·DILLAWAY·HOUSE·1750-1752·
ELIOT·SQUARE·ROXBURY·MASSACHUSETTS·

Measured & Drawn by Frank Chouteau Brown October 1932

Lower Part of Gallery Posts

Landing Post

Stair Base

Stair End ⅓ Full Size

Section A-A
Rail 2¾ x 3⅜

Newel 33″

2½ Sq

7 Sq

17 Turned

6⅜ Turned

bc

Tread 12″
Rise 7″

0 1 2 3 4 5 6 in. Inch Scale for Stair End.
Foot Scale for Elevation.
0 1 2 3 Ft. Inch Scale for Details.

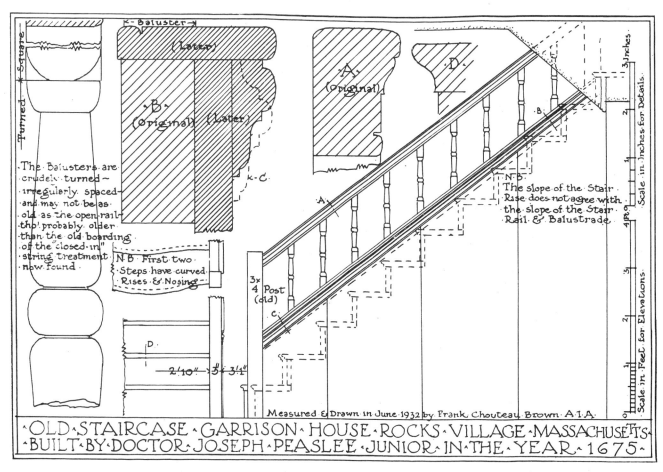

Turned   Square

Baluster

B (Later)
B (Original) (Later)

A (Original)

D

The Balusters are crudely turned ~ irregularly spaced and may not be as old as the open-rail — tho' probably older than the old boarding of the "closed-in" string treatment now found.

N B First two Steps have curved Rises & Nosing

3 x 4 Post (old)

N.B. The slope of the Stair Rise does not agree with the slope of the Stair Rail & Balustrade.

2′ 10″   5″ 3¼″

Scale in Feet for Elevations.
Scale in Inches for Details.

Measured & Drawn in June 1932 by Frank Chouteau Brown A.I.A.

·OLD·STAIRCASE·GARRISON·HOUSE·ROCKS·VILLAGE·MASSACHUSETTS·
·BUILT·BY·DOCTOR·JOSEPH·PEASLEE·JUNIOR·IN·THE·YEAR·1675·

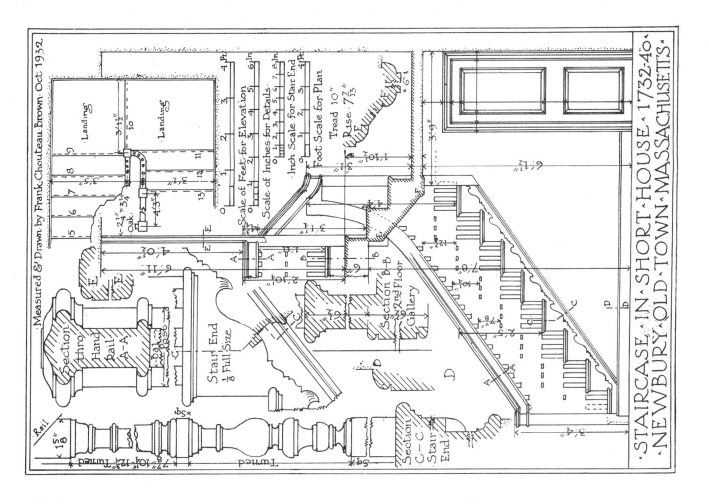

Measured & Drawn by Frank Chouteau Brown · Oct 1932

Landing

Landing

Section thro' Hand Rail A–A

Stair End ⅛ Full Size

Section C–C Stair End

Scale of Feet for Elevation
Scale of Inches for Details
Inch Scale for Details
Foot Scale for Plan
Tread 10"
Rise 7⅓

Section B–B 2nd Floor Gallery

Turned

Rail

Turned

· STAIRCASE · IN · SHORT · HOUSE · 1732-40 ·
· NEWBURY · OLD · TOWN · MASSACHUSETTS ·

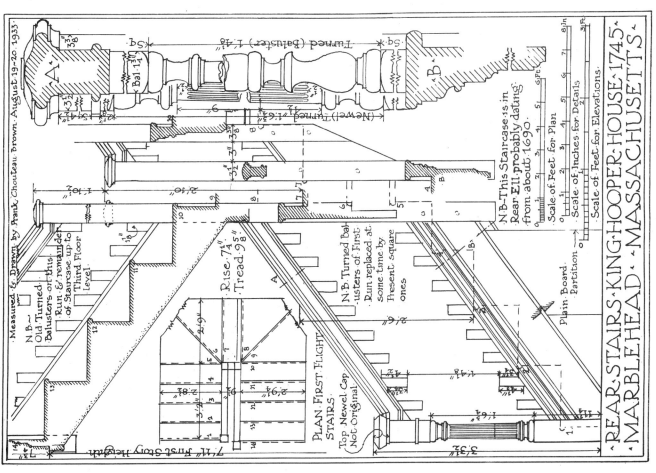

Measured & Drawn by Frank Chouteau Brown · August 19-20 · 1933 ·

N·B·~ Old-Turned Balusters on this Run & remainder of Staircase up to Third Floor level.

Turned (Baluster) 1:48

(Newel) Turned 1:6⅓

Rise 7¼"
Tread 9⅝"

N·B·Turned Balusters of First Run replaced at some time by present square ones

Plain Board Partition

N·B-This Staircase is in Rear Ell probably dating from about 1690.

Scale of Feet for Plan
Scale of Inches for Details
Scale of Feet for Elevations.

PLAN · FIRST · FLIGHT · STAIRS.

Top Newel Cap Not Original

First Story Height

· REAR · STAIRS · KING · HOOPER · HOUSE · 1745 ·
· MARBLEHEAD · MASSACHUSETTS ·

DILLAWAY STAIRCASE—1750-52—ROXBURY, MASS.

JOSEPH PEASLEE
STAIRCASE—1675—ROCK VILLAGE, MASS.

SHORT STAIRCASE—1732-40—NEWBURY OLD TOWN, MASS.

KING HOOPER REAR STAIRS—1745—MARBLEHEAD, MASS.

WILLIAM WATERS STAIRCASE
—1684—MARBLEHEAD, MASS.

GOV. JOHN WENTWORTH STAIRCASE
—1760—PORTSMOUTH, N. H.

Measured·August·12·&·Drawn·August·18·1933·by·Frank·Chouteau·Brown·A·I·A

·WEST·WINDOW·&·WALL·ON·STAIRCASE·LANDING·
·JEREMIAH·LEE·MANSION·1768·MARBLEHEAD·MASS·

208

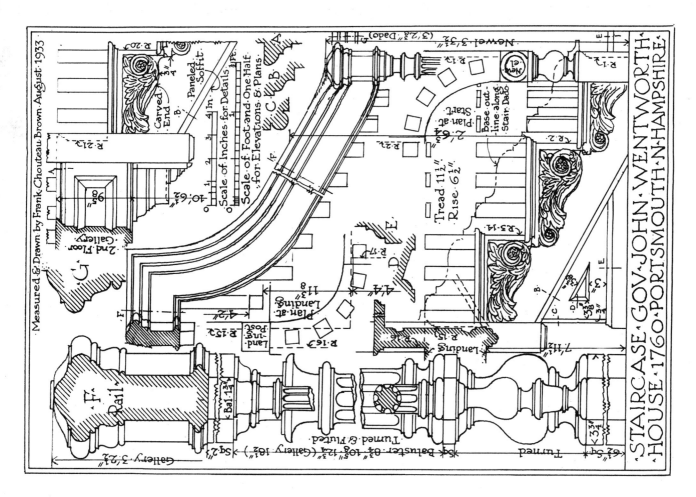

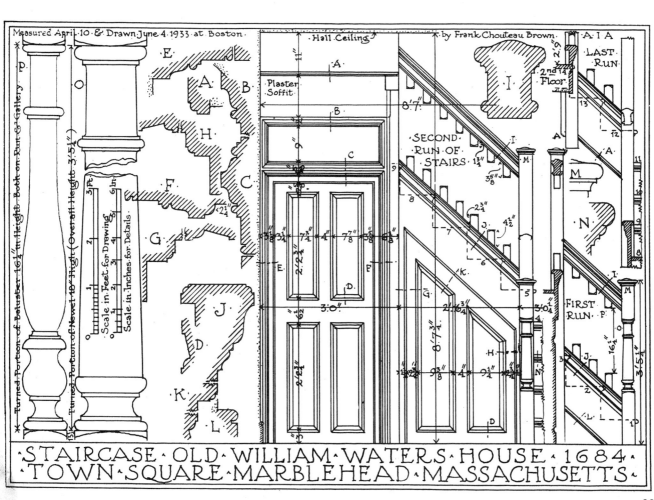

STAIRCASE·OLD·WILLIAM·WATERS·HOUSE·1684·
TOWN·SQUARE·MARBLEHEAD·MASSACHUSETTS·

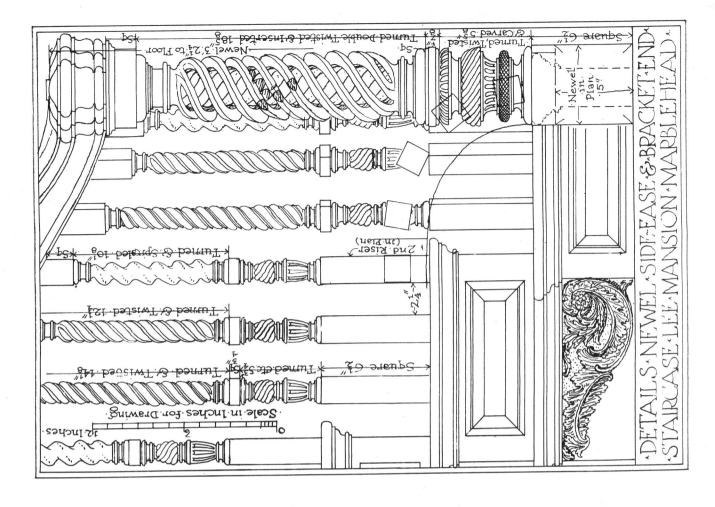

DETAILS·NEWEL·SIDE·EASE·&·BRACKET END·
·STAIRCASE·LEE·MANSION·MARBLEHEAD·

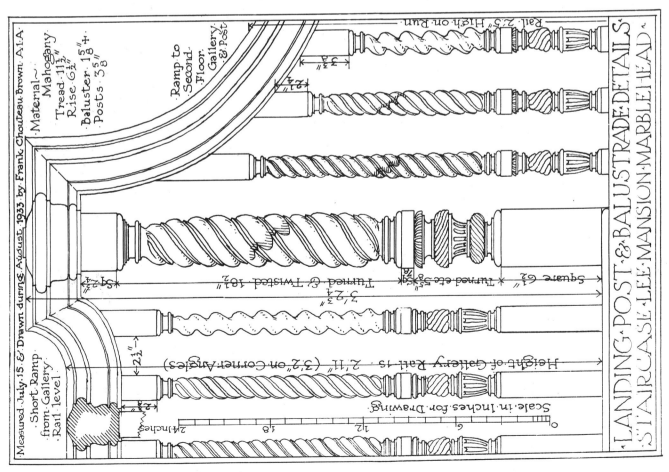

·LANDING·POST·&·BALUSTRADE·DETAILS·
·STAIRCASE·LEE·MANSION·MARBLEHEAD·

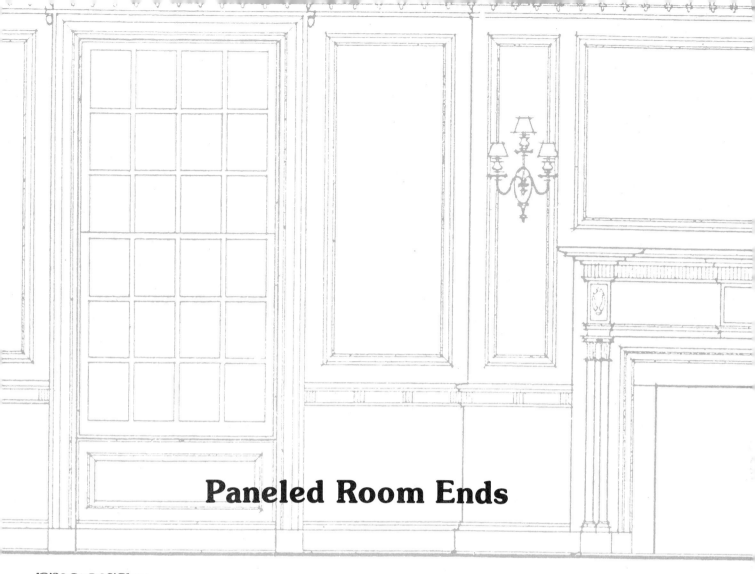

Paneled Room Ends

THE general prevalence of the paneled wall along one side of the room interior, where the fireplace is located, is widely established in most residential structures of the Seventeenth and Eighteenth Centuries in New England. Its origin derives from the principal type-plan of the one-room with fireplace at one end, or the two-room floor plan with the central chimney, that is almost universally found employed in early dwellings in that region. In either case, three sides of the room were along the exterior wall of the building.

A house built before 1660 by one of the wealthiest men in the Plymouth Colony, when taken down, revealed that the original oak frame was covered with one and one-eighth inch, wide oak boards, extending from the sill to the plate for the full two stories of the dwelling's height, with wide "shadow mouldings" along both edges of the inside face of the boards. They were indubitably intended to be exposed as the finish wall of the rooms inside.

This same sort of construction was used in Connecticut, in a building of as late date as 1820, where, however, the space between the rough natural edges of the boarding was plugged with lime mortar, and then split lathing nailed against the inner face of the wall and finish-coated with plaster.

On the other hand, both in that State and in Massachusetts, as well as others in New England, we have the early custom of placing the original split oak clapboards directly upon the exterior uprights of the old oak frames (without the use of any exterior boarding), the wall facing of the room inside being then either plastered on split laths, often six to eight feet long, nailed to the inner face of the frame; or sometimes faced on the interior with wide horizontal pine boarding, with feather-edge or lapped joints. An instance of a dwelling, built in 1649, illustrates the former method. In that particular case, the space between the studs was filled with puddled clay, probably from the inside as the split lath boards were added course over course. The clay was fluid enough to work out and fill up the spaces between the lapping oak rived clapboards, which were probably also plugged up with moist clay from the exterior, to insulate the wall and keep it tight against weather and cold.

On the face of the fourth, or inner wall of the room, the problem that confronted the early builders was entirely different. Here they were only concerned with surfacing the wall so that the unsightly bulk and

Paneled End in Southwest Bedroom
COL. WILLIAM R. LEE HOUSE—1745—
MARBLEHEAD, MASSACHUSETTS

Pine Paneled Wall in Southwest Room, First Floor
CAPTAIN SAMUEL TREVETT HOUSE—
c.1750—MARBLEHEAD, MASSACHUSETTS

(Historic American Buildings Survey)

PANELED END IN NORTHWEST BEDROOM
JEREMIAH LEE MANSION—1768—
MARBLEHEAD, MASSACHUSETTS

PANELED END IN NORTHEAST ROOM, FIRST FLOOR
CAPTAIN SAMUEL TREVETT HOUSE
MARBLEHEAD, MASSACHUSETTS
(*Built about 1750*)

GRAINED AND PANELED END IN SOUTHWEST ROOM, FIRST FLOOR
SQUIRE WILLIAM SEVER HOUSE—1760—KINGSTON, MASSACHUSETTS

rough clay daubing of the chimney stack would be concealed, but at the same time so that all the heat from flues and fireplaces would be left to radiate through the interior of the dwelling on all its floors and attic, for its full height. And as the need for fuller insulation against the cold New England winters became more and more important with each succeeding generation, the better insulation of plaster came to be accepted for use inside all the exterior walls of the dwelling (especially as limerock sources were discovered and worked more generally in the different settlements), while the transmittal of heat through the open pores of the wooden walls upon each side of the chimney stack and its clustering fireplaces was also generally appreciated. This was especially true before the painting of interior woodwork became fashionable. This period seems to vary in different sections, the earlier dates being about 1750, while many interiors are known to have been left in the natural wood, without paint, up to as late as a hundred years later. As the earlier paints used resembled rather thin pigment stains, they did little to fill the pores of the woods or prevent the passage of heat. But with the general use of heavier pigments, such as lead, of course the wood pores were entirely closed.

It should also be remembered that much of the paneling now found in early houses was not installed at the date given for the original construction of the dwelling, but in most cases was added many years later. The use of wide pine boards with feather or grooved edges for covering room walls was general in New England during the Seventeenth Century.

PORTION OF PANELED END IN OLD "HALL"
EMERY HOUSE—1675—
WEST NEWBURY, MASSACHUSETTS

215

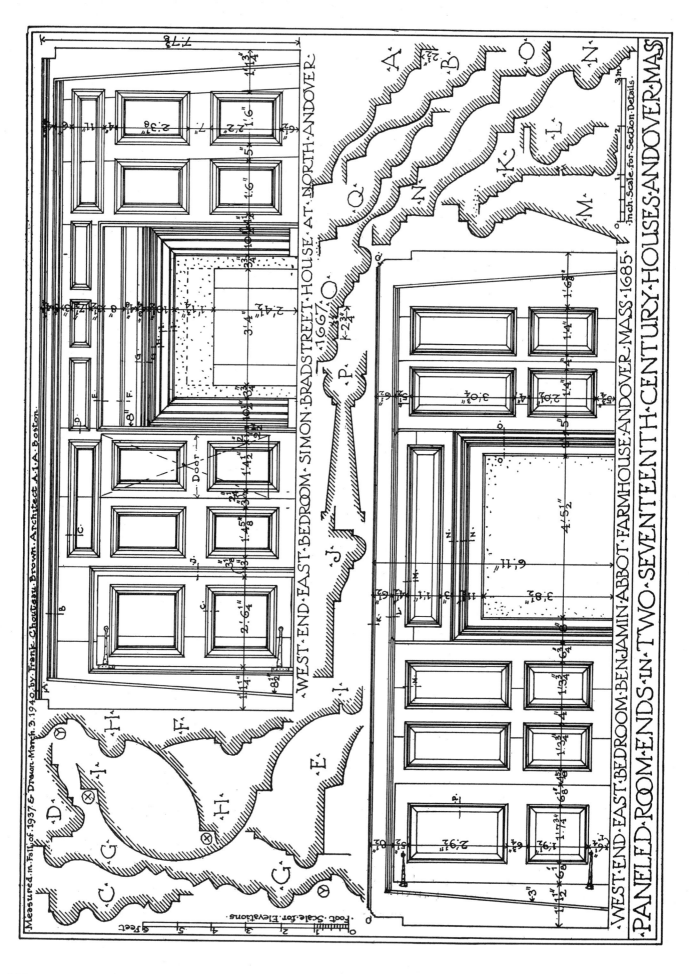

·WEST·END·EAST·BEDROOM·SIMON·BRADSTREET·HOUSE·AT·NORTH·ANDOVER·
·1667·

Measured·in·Fall·of·1937·&·Drawn·March·3·1940·by·Frank·Chouteau·Brown·Architect·A·I·A·Boston·

Foot·Scale·for·Elevations

·WEST·END·EAST·BEDROOM·BENJAMIN·ABBOT·FARMHOUSE·ANDOVER·MASS·1685·

·PANELED·ROOM·ENDS·IN·TWO·SEVENTEENTH·CENTURY·HOUSES·ANDOVER·MASS

Inch·Scale·for·Section·Details·

Paneled End, West Side of East Bedroom   *(Historic American Buildings Survey)*
SIMON BRADSTREET HOUSE—1667—NORTH ANDOVER, MASSACHUSETTS

Paneled End, West Side of East Bedroom
BENJAMIN ABBOT FARMHOUSE—1685—ANDOVER, MASSACHUSETTS
(Historic American Buildings Survey)

PORTION OF PANELED END, LIVING ROOM
COL. COOKE HOUSE—before 1730—
TIVERTON, R. I.

EARLY WOODWORK, SOUTH END OF
KITCHEN BEDROOM BRYANT-CUSHING
HOUSE—1698—NORWELL, MASS.
(Historic American Buildings Survey)

Near the end of that period—or early in the years that followed, raised panels, placed against the face of framed stiles, and held in position by some sort of bolection-shaped moulding, are frequently found, and in some sections this style is seen in dwellings built even after 1750. But meanwhile, the use of tall narrow panels, with a wide rail to stiffen the wall just below the middle of its height, began to supplant earlier methods, or even, in many cases, was applied upon the face of earlier paneling. This became the most prevalent and generally used style, extending up nearly to the end of that century. Following this usage, the four walls of the rooms were more and more generally all plastered, and the Georgian type of mantel, with shelf and overmantel extending up to the room cornice, became the fashion, until the overmantel itself came to be discontinued shortly after the beginning of the Nineteenth Century.

The illustrations show a few examples of the earliest type of boarded wall surfacing that still remain unsullied by the addition of later paint coatings. Following this, came walls with applied or raised panels. This required a heavy moulding, that continued into later years as an emphasis to the overmantel panel. Then came another form of covering border moulding; and, finally, the simpler panel moulding most commonly and widely used, which appears in many other New England

(Historic American Buildings Survey)

PANELED FIREPLACE WALL IN OLD LIVING ROOM
CUSHING HOUSE—1720—HINGHAM, MASSACHUSETTS

wall treatments. It is also characteristic that all the effect of this type of paneling is obtained without the use of any separate strip of moulding. The quarter-round itself is run along the inner edge of the framed enclosing stiles, and the thin sloping border running around all four sides of the enclosed panel, intended to fit into the grooved edge of the stile, itself functionally completes the raised moulding panel section.

With one exception, 1760 is about the latest date of the houses whose interior wall treatments have been illustrated, and in later dwellings, of course, the paneling is far more likely to have been installed as part of the original finish. It is in the earlier dwellings that later interior paneled walls and mantels, and casing over of early structural beams and posts, are usually found.

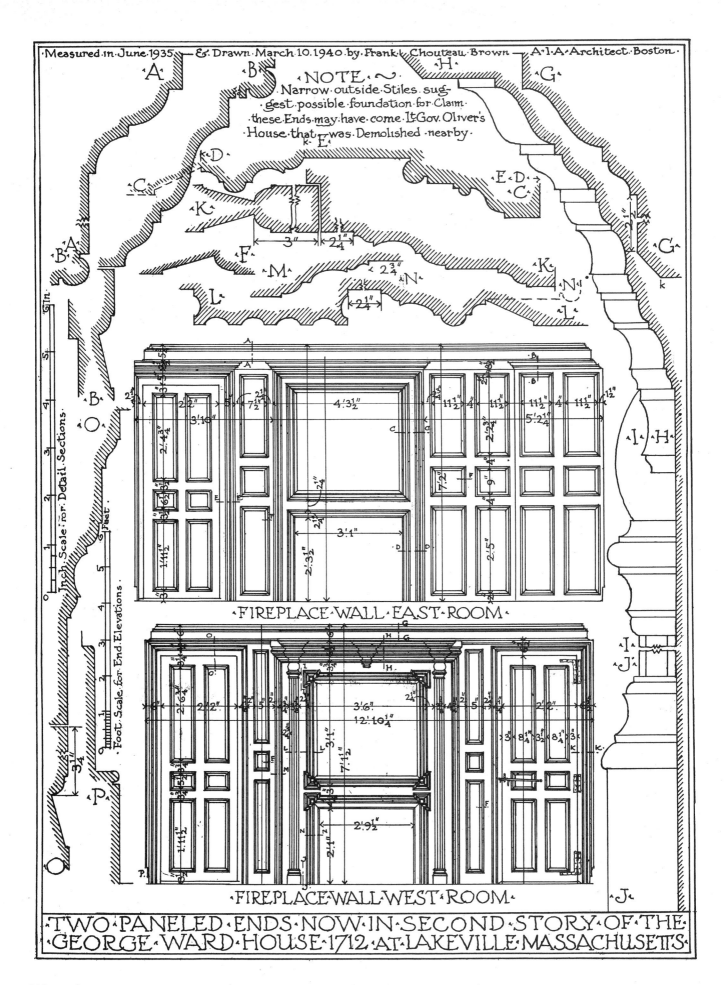

Measured in June 1935 — & Drawn March 10 1940 by Frank Chouteau Brown — A·I·A·Architect·Boston·

·NOTE·~

Narrow·outside·Stiles·suggest·possible·foundation·for·Claim·these·Ends·may·have·come·Lt·Gov·Oliver's·House·that·was·Demolished·nearby·

·FIREPLACE·WALL·EAST·ROOM·

·FIREPLACE·WALL·WEST·ROOM·

·TWO·PANELED·ENDS·NOW·IN·SECOND·STORY·OF·THE·
·GEORGE·WARD·HOUSE·1712·AT·LAKEVILLE·MASSACHUSETTS·

PANELED END IN SOUTHWEST PARLOR
GEN. JOSEPH L. DWIGHT HOUSE—1759—
GREAT BARRINGTON, MASSACHUSETTS

H.A.B.S.

PANELED END IN WEST BEDROOM
GEORGE WARD HOUSE—1712—
LAKEVILLE, MASSACHUSETTS

Portion of Paneled End in Southwest Room, First Floor
JUDGE JOSEPH LEE-NICHOLS HOUSE—c.1660—
CAMBRIDGE, MASSACHUSETTS